참선이란 무엇인가?

마음의 고향에 이르는 길

WHAT IS SEON?

The Path that Leads Home

참선이란 무엇인가?

초판 1쇄 2016년 8월 15일
　　8쇄 2021년 11월 12일

지은이 진제 대선사　**옮긴이** 박희원·진우기·홍연주　**감수** June Park·진우기·도민 스님
펴낸이 서정희　**펴낸곳** 매경출판㈜　**후원** 진제선회
등　록 2003년 4월 24일(No. 2-3759)
주　소 우)04557 서울시 중구 충무로 2(필동1가) 매일경제 별관 2층 매경출판㈜
홈페이지 www.mkbook.co.kr
전　화 02)2000-2612(기획편집)　02)2000-2636(마케팅)　02)2000-2606(구입 문의)
팩　스 02)2000-2609　**이메일** publish@mk.co.kr
인쇄·제본 ㈜M-print　031)8071-0961

ISBN 979-11-5542-452-0(03810)
값 16,000원

참선이란 무엇인가?

마음의 고향에 이르는 길

대한불교조계종 종정
진제 대선사의 가르침

WHAT IS SEON?

The Path that Leads Home

TEACHINGS OF GREAT SEON MASTER JINJE,
THE SUPREME PATRIARCH OF THE JOGYE ORDER OF KOREAN BUDDHISM

매일경제신문사

화두

HWADU

부모에게 나기 전에 어떤 것이 참나인가?

"What is your true self
before you are born of your parents?"

THE SUPREME PATRIARCH OF THE JOGYE ORDER
OF KOREAN BUDDHISM

대한불교조계종 종정 진제법원 대선사
Great Seon Master Jinje Beopwon, the Supreme Patriarch of the Jogye Order of Korean Buddhism

광화문 대법회장 광경
광복 70주년 한반도 통일과 세계 평화를 위한 세계 간화선 무차대법회, 2015

The Conference for World Peace and Reunification of Korea
The Great Equality Assembly of Ganhwa Seon at Gwanghwamun Plaza (Seoul, 2015)

종정 예하 상당법문
광복 70주년 한반도 통일과 세계 평화를 위한 세계 간화선 무차대법회, 2015

His Eminence Jinje Giving a Dharma Talk
Conference for World Peace and Reunification of Korea
Great Equality Assembly of Ganhwa Seon (Seoul, 2015)

세계종교지도자들과 현충원 참배
광복 70주년 한반도 통일과 세계 평화를 위한 세계 간화선 무차대법회, 2015

The World Religious Leaders Visit Seoul National Cemetery
The Conference for World Peace and Reunification of Korea

종정 예하께서 창건하신 남해 성담사 전경

Seongdamsa Temple in Namhae-gun, Gyeongsangnam-do

종정 예하께서 창건하신 부산 해운정사 전경

Haeunjeong-sa Temple in Mt. Jangsu-san, Haeundae, Busan City

추천사

東堂 성낙인
서울대학교 총장

　서양에서 기독교가 그러하듯이, 불교는 그 자체로 한국의 역사이자 한국인의 사상적 근원이다. 유럽에서 기독교가 로마교황청 휘하의 신정일치에서 점차 개별국가의 독립으로 이어진 것과는 반대로 한국불교는 태생적으로 호국불교에 터 잡아 국태민안을 기원해 왔다. 해인사 팔만대장경은 이를 웅변으로 보여준다.
　인간의 삶, 인생, 생명, 행복, 죽음이란 무엇인가? 이 모든 화두(話頭)의 근원을 찾아가는 과정에 불가의 선(禪)이 자리 잡고 있다. 우리나라 선종의 맥을 이은 대한불교 조계종의 큰 어른이신 진제 종정께서는 선의 세계를 사부대중에게 펼쳐 보이고 계신다. 종정께서는 한국 선맥의 중흥조인 경허 대선사로부터 혜월, 운봉, 향곡 대선사에 이르는 법맥을 잇고 있다. 불교에서 수행의 방안에는 경전을 독송하는 간경, 주문을 외우는 주력, 좌선을 통하여 깨침을 추구하는 참선이 있다. 이 중에서 선종은 참선 수행의 맥을 잇는다.
　속인이 선의 세계를 범접하기는 결코 쉬운 일이 아니다. 더구나 한국불교의 오랜 논쟁사안인 돈오점수(頓悟漸修)를 뛰어넘는 돈오돈수(頓悟頓修)의 근본적인 문제에서는 더욱 그렇다. 나는 오래 전

성철 종정이 일거에 진리의 세계를 터득하여야 한다는 돈오돈수를 강조하신 것을 기억한다.

당시만 해도 혈기왕성한 젊은 나이였던 나는 학문이란《논어》의 '학이시습지 불역열호'(學而時習之 不亦說乎)'라는 구절처럼 익히고 또 익혀서 널리 지식의 세계를 탐구하는 것이라고 생각했던 터라 도무지 대선사의 돈오돈수를 이해할 수 없었다. 하지만 이순을 훌쩍 넘어서고 보니 서서히 깨닫는 것도 중요하지만, 깨달음의 경지는 예고된 것이 아니라 어느 날 불현듯 닥쳐 올 수 있다는 명제에 기울게 된다.

'마음의 고향에 이르는 길'이라는 책의 부제는 수도는 결국 자기 자신의 문제로 귀착됨을 의미한다. 대선사께서는 책 속에서 "부모에게 나기 전에 어떤 것이 참나인고?"라는 화두를 던지고 계신다.

진제 종정께서는 한국불교가 산중에 머무르지 않고 대중에게 다가갈 수 있도록 크게 기여하고 계신다. 이는 광복 70주년 한반도 통일과 세계 평화를 위한 세계 간화선 무차(無遮)대법회상당법어에도 드러나 있다. "마음이 곧 부처요, 사람이 곧 부처"임을 설파하시면서 "번뇌에 미혹할 때는 고해의 사바세계가 있으나, 참나를 깨달으면 시방이 공하여 고통스러운 현실에서 곧바로 해탈열반(解脫涅槃)의 삶을 실현하는 지름길"이 된다고 말씀하신 것이다.

종정께서는 이를 위해 '보시, 지계, 인욕, 정진, 선정, 지혜'라는 여섯 가지 덕목을 제시한다. 오늘을 살아가는 현대인 모두가 생활철학으로 삼아야 할 소중한 경구이다. 이는 종정께서 책 말미에 제시하신 '인성오계'와도 일맥상통한다. "첫째는 국가와 사회에 필요한 사람이 됩시다. 둘째는 부모와 조상님께 효도합시다. 셋째는 친구와 이웃을 사귐에 있어 서로 신의와 사랑으로 합시다. 넷째는 맡은 바 일에 있어서 성실과 정성을 다합시다. 다섯째는 대자비심을 가지고 뭇 생명을 존중합시다."

종정께서 설파하신 법어는 내가 서울대 총장 취임사에서 '선(善)한 인재'의 양성을 통해서 우리 사회가 공동선과 공동체적 가치를 소중히 여기는 '선한 사람들의 공동체'가 되기를 기원한 바와 그 맥락을 같이 한다.

끝으로 책에는 오늘의 질박한 삶에서 마음의 평화를 찾기 위한 간화선(看話禪) 수행법이 제시되어 있다. "아침저녁으로 좌복 위에 반가부좌를 하고 앉아 허리를 곧게 하고 가슴을 편 다음 두 손을 모아서 단전에다 붙입니다. 눈은 2미터 아래에다 화두생각을 두고 응시하되, 혼침과 망상에 떨어지지 않도록 눈을 뜨고 의심에 몰두해야 합니다."

《참선이란 무엇인가?》의 특별한 의미는 무엇보다도 알 듯 모를 듯한 불교사상 특히 선의 세계를 가까이 접할 수 있는 기회를 제공하는 데 있다. 이는 책을 관통하는 기본흐름에서도 잘 드러난다. 고답적이고 낯선 언어의 유희 같은 선불교의 세계가 오늘을 살아가는 우리 모두가 갈구하는 삶인 호국불교, 국태민안, 세계 평화로 들어오는 것을 체감할 수 있다.

특히 오늘날 정신적으로나 물질적으로나 힘들어하는 젊은이들에게《참선이란 무엇인가?》는 삶의 소중한 양식을 부담 없이 얻을 양서라 아니할 수 없다. 다른 세계의 언어 같은 고승들의 한문 법어를 알기 쉬운 한글로 잘 정리하였을 뿐만 아니라 영문 번역까지 곁들여 놓아 일독을 권할 만하다. 이 책이 한국불교의 대중화를 뛰어넘어 세계화를 위한 소중한 밑거름이 되리라 확신한다.

Preface

Sung Nak In
Chancellor of Seoul National University

Just as Christianity has in the West, Buddhism has become the very foundation and ideological basis of Korea. The Eastern Orthodox Church gradually gained independence from what was once a unified whole in the Roman Catholic Church.

Korean Buddhism, however, originated from a form of "patriotic Buddhism" that promoted the wellbeing of the nation. The establishment of the Tripitaka Koreana now housed in Haein-sa Temple is a very good demonstration of this.

What are life, living, existence, happiness and death? In the process of understanding the basis of *hwadu* meditation, Seon Buddhism will be revealed. Master Jinje, supreme patriarch of the Jogye Order of Korean Buddhism, is the current lineage holder of orthodox Seon Buddhism. And for Korean Buddhism's fourfold assembly, he is the gateway to Seon practice. He continues the principal lineage that once was carried forward by such eminent masters as Gyeongheo,

Hyewol, Unbong, Hyanggok and Seogu. Buddhist practices often include recitation of Buddhist sutras, chanting of mantra or dharani, and sitting meditation to attain enlightenment. In the case of orthodox Seon Buddhism, sitting meditation is the main spiritual practice.

Understanding the world of Seon is not easy for lay practitioners. In Korean Buddhism, the arguments on sudden enlightenment and gradual cultivation (jeomsu) vs. sudden enlightenment and cultivation (donsu) have been quite apparent from its early days. Seon Master Seongcheol, former supreme patriarch of the Jogye Order, emphasized "dono donsu" which teaches that the realization of truth must come suddenly and in an instant. I did not understand his teachings in the past, as I was young and passionate, blinded by desire for intellectual knowledge. But now that I am over sixty, I have begun to pay attention not only to attaining realization but to understanding that the path to realization is never predictable and can come suddenly at any moment without notice.

As inferred in the title, "What is Seon?: the Path that Leads Home," the practice and the path are ultimately what one must face alone.

Great Seon Master Jinje asks the question, "What is your true self before you are born of your parents?"

Seon Master Jinje propagates Buddhism to the general public so that Korean Buddhism does not remain simply locked away in mountain temples. It is also demonstrated in his Dharma Talk at the Conference for World Peace and Reunification of Korea: The Great Equality Assembly of Ganhwa Seon.

He taught that a mind is Buddha and a person is also a Buddha.

"When you are deluded by your mental afflictions, you will experience the suffering of the secular world. However, when you attain your true self, the ten directions are empty and open to you. You can then swiftly transform painful reality into a life of liberation." He showed six paths we should take to attain this: generosity, ethics, patience, joyous effort, meditation and wisdom.

These are particularly important for people today as daily values, and they parallel the five virtues of character development he teaches in his book. First, make a positive contribution to society. Second, honor your parents and respect your elders. Third, build worthy friendships in love and trust. Fourth, be sincere and earnest in carrying out your responsibilities. Fifth, respect all life with love and compassion.

This Dharma Talk is similar to a speech I made on how to cultivate noble citizens during my inauguration as chancellor. The speech was in the context of improving our society and developing a community of respectable people for the common good.

Lastly, Master Jinje teaches Ganhwa Seon practice for today's world in order for people to find peace in their lives.

"To practice Ganhwa Seon, sit comfortably on your cushion every morning and evening. Straighten your back, expand your chest, and place both hands on your lap below your navel. Look toward the floor six feet in front of you and focus your single-minded concentration on your *hwadu*. Keep your eyes open so that you don't succumb to drowsiness or distracting thoughts."

The reason I recommend the book, "What is Seon?" is in the hope that people become better acquainted with often challenging Buddhist philosophy, especially Seon Buddhism. The teachings are carefully revealed in the way this book is designed. The strange expressions and high-toned literary styles often seen in Seon Buddhism still relate to the idealistic life we long for, patriotic Buddhism, national prosperity and world peace.

Especially for youths facing mental and physical struggles,

this book will provide important teachings on the important values in life. Making the book available in both Korean and English allows people to better understand difficult ancient Chinese. I am certain that this book not only provides a valuable foundation for popularizing Korean Buddhism but goes beyond that in propagating Korean Buddhism to the rest of the world.

추천사

조갑제
조갑제닷컴 대표

이 책은 眞際 대선사의 불교 중흥 선언이다!
한국불교의 나아갈 길(통일)과 방도(참선수행)을 제시하였다

圓空身體

수년 전 겨울, 눈 내리는 날이었다. 사람을 통하여 眞際 大禪師(진제 대선사)가 나를 만나고 싶다는 말을 전해 듣고 대구 棟華寺로 가서 스님의 강론을 듣고 이야기를 나누었다. 참선수행을 강조하면서 "이 세상에 태어나지 않은 셈 치고 그 법을 구해보지 않겠느냐?"라던 말이 머리에 오래 남았지만, 그 말보다도 大禪師의 풍채가 압도적이었다.

대선사의 대칭적이고 원만한 모습에서 문득 '圓空身體(원공신체)'라는 낱말이 떠올랐다. 경주박물관에 있는 新羅 聖德大王新鐘(신라 성덕대왕신종)은 별명이 奉德寺鐘(봉덕사종)이고 속칭은 에밀레종이다. 이 종에 새겨진 640여 字의 頌詞(송사)가 있고 '圓空身體'라는 말이 나온다. 이 梵鐘은 그냥 종이 아니라 그 형상이 둥글고 속이 비어 있으므로 바로 '神의 몸'을 상징한다는 뜻이다.

神의 속성을 圓空, 즉 둥글고 속이 빈 존재로 규정한 것이 참으로 의미 깊다. 원만하면서도 속이 비어 있는 사람을 상상해보라. 그런 사람은 부처님을 닮은 사람이다. 둥글둥글해서 누구와도 싸우지 않으며 속이 텅 비어 있어 모든 것, 즉 갈등과 淸濁(청탁)까지도 다 받아들여 하나의 질서로 융합한다.

《참선이란 무엇인가?》를 나 읽고 나서 신제스님이 바로 그런 분이고, 看話禪(간화선)의 수행법으로 모든 사람들이 그 경지에 도달할 수 있다는 사실을 알게 되었다.

眞際 - Moment of truth

나는 평생을 글로써 먹고 산 사람이라 作名(작명)에 관심이 많다. 大禪師를 만나고 돌아와서 '眞際'라는 法號(법호)의 뜻에 대하여 한동안 생각해보곤 하였는데 《참선이란 무엇인가?》를 읽으니 답이 있었다.

<향곡 선사께서 "옳고 옳다" 하시며, 臨濟正脈(임제정맥)의 法燈(법등)을 咐囑(부촉)하시고 眞際라는 法號와 함께 傳法偈(전법게)를 내리셨습니다. 이때가 1967년, 산승(山僧)의 나이 서른셋 되던 해였습니다.>

'眞際'는 참 眞과 때 際이니 진실의 시간이다. 際의 함축된 뜻은 11시 10분이란 식의 時刻(시각)이 아니라 時間(시간)의 개념으로서 '즈음'에 가깝다. 즉 '진실을 깨달을 즈음', 줄이면 '진실의 시간'이다. 영어에 'Moment of truth'라는 표현이 있는데 이게 眞際의 정확한 영문 번역일 것이다. 'Moment of truth'를 보통 '결정적 순간'이라고 번

역한다. 인간이 어떤 사물의 진실을 발견하는 순간은 그의 인생이나 역사에서 결정적 순간이 된다. 불교인들에겐 '得道(득도)의 순간'으로 설명하는 게 나을 것이다.

眞際! 참으로 잘 지은 이름이다. 부처님과 조사님들이 남긴 '看話禪'의 맥을 잇고 있는(대선사가 이 책에서 설명하는 바로는 한국이 세계에서 유일하게 정통의 맥을 계승하고 있다) 큰 스님의 이름으로는 이보다 더 좋을 수가 없으리라.

대선사는 이렇게 자부한다.

"부처님과 조사스님들께서는 바로 이러한 甚深微妙(심심미묘)한 見性法(견성법)을 전하고 전하신 것이며, 그 견성법이 오직 한 가닥 이곳 한국에 머물러 있는 것입니다."

凡夫가 위대한 부처가 되는 법

경남 남해에서 출생한 진제 스님은 가까운 해관암에서 石友(석우) 선사를 만난 것이 자신의 운명을 바꾸었다고 썼다.

石友 禪師는 山僧(眞際 선사)에게 "세상의 생활도 좋지만 그보다 더 값진 삶이 있으니, 네가 한번 해보지 않겠느냐?"고 말한다.

"무엇이 그리 값진 삶입니까?"

"凡夫가 위대한 부처되는 법이 있으니, 이 세상에 태어나지 않은 셈 치고 그 법을 구해보지 않겠느냐?"

진제스님은 이 제안을 받아들여 생애를 건 수행의 길에 나서 드디어 得道한다. '참나'를 깨달은 것이다. 그가 발견한 '참나'의 실체는 무엇인가? 이 책은 이 부분의 설명에 주안점을 두고 있다.

<참나를 깨닫는다고 하는 것은 지금 이 자리에서 山僧의 法門을 듣고 있는 여러분이 삶의 주인공임을 깨닫는 것입니다. 그 주인공은 모든 곳에서 주인공이 되어, 삶의 많은 부분을 無碍自在(무애자재)하게 수용할 수 있게 됩니다.

그래서 어디에도 의존하지 않고 모든 가치관에서 자유로운 사람이 되며, 모든 종교와 정치제도, 문화적 제약에서 벗어난 절대 자유인이 되는 것이니, 인류의 희망이 참나를 깨닫는 데 있고, 미래가 여기서 열리게 되는 것입니다. (中略) 이러한 정의와 행복과 자유와 지혜와 평등은 아무리 학식이 풍부하고, 아무리 부유하고, 아무리 지위와 명성이 높고 성스럽게 산다 할지라도 누릴 수 있는 것이 아닙니다. 오직 참나를 깨달은 자만이 누릴 수 있는 것입니다.

죽음에 다다라서도 밝은 마음, 맑은 정신으로 옷 갈아입듯 벗게 되고, 다음 생에는 반드시 진리를 깨닫게 될 것입니다. 그러나 이러한 參禪(참선) 수행을 등한시 한다면 온갖 분별과 시비와 갈등에 하루뿐만 아니라 一生을 헛되게 보내게 될 것이니, 그 결과는 고통과 갈등뿐이라서 죽음에 다다라 후회한들 이미 늦습니다.>

참나를 깨달은 사람은 행동에서 주체적 인간이 되는데 그는 거침이 없는 자유자재의 인간, 즉 절대 자유인이다. 그런 사람이 바로 부처인 셈이다.

진제스님은 그 어려운 수행의 방도를 여러 가지 例話(예화)를 들어 설명한다.

<어떻게 닦는 것이 바른 참선 수행인가? 話頭(화두)가 있는 이는 각자 話頭를, 없는 이는 "부모에게 나기 전에 어떤 것이 참나인가" 하고 일상생활 속에서 마음에서 우러나오는 간절한 마음으로 寤寐不忘(오매불망) 의심하는 것입니다.>

광화문에서

2015년 5월 16일 해방 70주년을 맞아 서울 광화문에서 열렸던 <한반도 통일과 세계 평화를 위한 기원대회(세계 看話禪 무차대법회)>에서 眞際 대종사가 설파한 法語(법어)는 깊고 넓은 스케일의 말씀이다.

"온갖 亡靈(망령)된 생각들을 즉각 내려놓는다면, 바로 그 자리가 본래의 마음자리며 본래의 참모습인 것입니다. 迷惑(미혹)하면 衆生(중생)이요, 항상 밝아 있으면 부처이기에, 凡夫와 聖人(성인)이 근본 자리에서는 둘이 아님이요, 그대로 광명이요, 생명이요, 평화요, 大自由(대자유)입니다. 그렇기에 누구든지 참나를 깨달으면 영원한 행복과 大智慧(대지혜)를 누릴 수 있는 것입니다.

그러므로 마음이 곧 부처요, 사람이 곧 부처라고 말하는 것입니다. 이렇게 사람이 곧 부처임을 깨달아서 서로 존중하고 相生(상생)하는 삶을 만드는 일이 이 자리에 있는 우리가 이루어야 할 誓願(서원)입니다. 옛 聖人이 말씀하시기를 '가는 곳마다 주인이 되면, 서 있는 그 자리가 모두 진리의 세계'라고 했습니다. 모든 번뇌망상을 놓아버리고 참나를 깨달아 세상의 주인이 되면 언제 어디서나 걸림 없는 大自在의 삶을 살게 됩니다."

'참나'를 自覺(자각)하면 거침없는 자유자재의 삶을 살게 되고 森羅萬象(삼라만상)의 진정한 주인이 된다. 내 운명의 주인이고, 역사의 주인이며, 우주의 주인이 된다. 이것이 진정한 인간해방일 것이다. 參禪의 방법은 고독하고 고립적인 행동이지만 그 결과는 大乘的(대승적)이고, 세속적이며, 인간의 구원이다.

한국불교, 통일을 말하다

수년 전 눈 내리는 날 동화사에서 만난 眞際 대선사는 나에게 한반도 통일을 話頭로 던졌고, 나는 한국불교가 신라 통일기의 호국불교와 같은 역할을 해주었으면 한다는 희망을 전하였다.

작년 광화문에 雲集한 수십만의 불교인들은 <한반도 평화를 위한 2015 불교통일 선언>을 채택,<불교는 굳어져 버린 남북관계를 풀고 민족 동질성회복과 통일의 大業(대업)을 이룩하는 데 앞장서겠다>고 다짐하였다. 진제대선사는 "우리 모두가 수행을 일상화할 때 마음속에 있는 모든 갈등이 해소될 수 있다. 이러한 생각을 남북한 사람들의 마음에 심어주면 모든 시기와 질투, 분쟁이 사라질 것이라고 확신한다. 남북한의 통일도 더욱 빨리 실현될 것이다"라고 강조하였다.

통일 문제가 한국불교의 話頭로 채택된 셈이다. 진제 스님은 통일의 방도를 불교적으로 소화하여 설명한 것이다. 남북한의 중생들이 '참나'를 찾는 노력을 통하여 갈등과 분열을 극복하고 <마침내 마음

의 고향에 이르러 大自由와 大智慧와 大安樂(대안락) 그리고 大平和(대평화)를 영원토록 누리게 되는> 것이다.

한국불교의 가장 큰 역사적 偉業(위업)은 신라의 삼국통일이다. 화랑도의 행동 윤리인 世俗五戒(세속오계)를 제시한 圓光(원광), 통합의 원리를 실천한 元曉(원효), 통일전쟁의 후유증을 佛國化(불국화)로 극복하려 한 義湘(의상), 그리고 金春秋(김춘추), 金庾信(김유신), 金法敏(김법민), 화랑도. 이들 통일의 주역은 불교적 死生觀(사생관)과 세계관으로 뭉쳐서 三國을 한 나라로 만들고 한반도를 활동공간으로 삼아 韓民族(한민족)을 빚어내었으며 이는 우리가 살고 있는 이 대한민국의 터전이 되었다. 종교와 국가의 관계가 헝클어지면 나라도 민중도 종교도 고생하는데 신라에선 국가와 불교가 相生, 엄청난 생산력을 발휘하였다. 眞際 대선사는 1,300여 년 만에 다시 한 번 불교의 나아갈 방향(통일)과 방도(참나의 발견)를 제시한 셈이다. 이는 불교 중흥의 길이기도 하다.

金庾信의 자주정신

당시 세계 최강의 제국인 唐과 동맹하여 백제 고구려를 통합한 뒤 唐이 신라를 屬國化하려 하자 7년간의 大唐(대당)결전을 통하여 민족의 독립성을 확보한 신라는 '참나'를 발견한 주체적 인간들의 집단이었다. 불교적 자주성의 상징적 인물은 金庾信이다.

고려의 金富軾(김부식)은 《三國史記》에서 김유신을 '자주정신의 化身'이자 삼국시대 제1인물로 그렸다(別傳에 실린 그에 대한 기록은 어떤 왕에 대한 기록보다 상세하다).

서기 660년, 羅唐연합군이 백제를 멸망시킨 직후 蘇定方(소정방)의 唐軍(당군)이 신라마저 치려하자 金庾信은 대책회의에서 이렇게 주장한다.

"개는 그 주인을 두려워하지만 주인이 그 다리를 밟으면 무는 법입니다. 우리가 어려움을 당하였는데 어찌 스스로를 구원하지 않겠습니까."

신라가 결전 태세를 갖추자 蘇定方은 계획을 거두고 귀국, 唐 고종에게 보고를 하니 고종은 "왜 내친 김에 신라마저 치지 않았느냐"고 따진다. 金富軾은, 이 질문에 소정방이 이렇게 답하였다고 《三國史記》에 기록하였다.

"신라는 임금이 어질고 백성을 사랑하며 그 신하가 충성으로 나라를 섬기고 아랫사람은 윗사람 섬기기를 父兄(부형)과 같이 하니 비록 나라는 작지만 함부로 도모할 수가 없었습니다."

이 말은 唐의 최고장수가 신라에게 바친 찬사인 셈이다. 임금, 신하, 백성들이 自主의식으로 일치단결한 나라가 신라였다는 이야기이다. 이런 단결을 가능하게 만든 접착제가 불교정신이었을 것이다. 소정방의 말에서 유의할 부분이 있다.

그는 '신하가 충성으로 임금을 섬기고'라고 말하지 않고 '충성으로 나라를 섬기고'라고 말한다. 국가를 임금보다 높게 여기는 語法(어법)이다. 국가와 왕을 동일시한 것은 동양뿐 아니라 18세기 프랑스 대혁명 이전의 서양도 마찬가지였다. 하지만 신라인들은 국가를 임금보다 優位(우위)에 놓았다는 이야기가 된다. 이는 경이적인데 이 또한 불교의 보편적 가치관을 나타내는 게 아닐까?

殺生有擇의 고민

圓光은 신라 진평왕 시절 世俗五戒를 만들면서 '殺生有擇(살생유택)'을 넣고 왕을 위하여 乞師表(걸사표)를 써 隋나라에 도움을 요청한다. 불교의 승려가 해선 안 될 일이지만 存亡(존망)의 위기를 맞은 국가를 위하여 불교가 해야 할 일을 한 것이고 그리하여 護國(호국)불교라는 찬사를 받게 되었다. 원광은 진평왕의 부탁을 받아 걸사표를 지으면서 "자기가 살기 위하여 남을 멸하는 것은 승려로서의 행동이 아니나, 저는 대왕의 땅에서 살고 대왕의 물과 풀을 먹고 있으니 감히 명을 따르지 않겠습니까"라고 했다고 한다. 이런 고민이 만들어낸 것이 정치와 전쟁에까지 스며든 불교적 美學(미학)이다.

세속오계는 臨戰無退(임전무퇴)라는 尙武(상무)정신과 殺生有擇이란 불교정신이 절묘한 균형을 이룬다. 나라를 위하여 용감하게 싸우되 살생은 최소한에 그쳐야 한다는 것이다. 이런 근대적 합리성은 古代에선 어느 나라에서도 찾아보기 어렵다.

文武王(문무왕)도 이름 자체가 화랑도적 상무정신과 불교적 자비의 합성이다. 文武王의 文은 불교가 만들어낸 文的요소 -종교·예술·건축-의 상징이다. 문무왕은 삼국통일을 완성한 분인데, 그 힘이 文과 武의 통합에서 생겼음을 의미한다.

《三國史記》에 적혀 있는 통일대왕 文武王의 遺言(유언)은 죽음을 앞둔 권력자의 말로서는 세계역사상 유례가 없을 정도로 담담하다. 죽음을 맞아 모든 것을 비운 사람의 담백한 정신을 엿볼 수 있다.

<(前略) 山谷은 변하고 세대는 바뀌기 마련이다. 吳王(오왕, 손권)의 北山 무덤에 금으로 채색한 새를 볼 수 없고 魏主(위주, 조조)의 西陵(서릉)에는 오직 銅雀(동작)의 이름만 들을 뿐이라. 옛날 萬機(만기)를 다스리던 영웅도 마침내 한 무더기의 흙이 되고 만다. 草童(초동)목수는 그 위에서 노래하며, 여우토끼는 그 곁을 구멍 뚫는다. 한갓 자재를 낭비하여 虛事(허사)와 비방만을 책에 남기고, 헛되이 人力만 수고롭게 할 뿐 사람의 영혼을 구제할 수 없는 것이다. 고요히 생각하면 마음의 아픔을 금할 수 없으니 이와 같은 것들은 내가 즐겨하는 바 아니므로, 죽은 뒤 10일이 되면 庫門(고문)의 바깥뜰에서 印度(인도) 의식에 따라 화장하여 장사지내고, 服(복)의 輕重(경중)은 규정이 있으나 喪(상)의 제도는 애써 검약하게 하라. 邊城(변성)의 鎭守(진수)와 州(주), 縣(현)의 課稅(과세)도 꼭 필요치 아니하면 모두 헤아려서 폐하고, 율령과 격식 중 불편한 것이 있으면 곧 고치도록 하라. 사방에 포고하여 이 뜻을 널리 알게 하고, 소속 官員(관원)은 곧 시행하라.>

문무왕의 인간됨을 느끼게 해주는 이 유언은 천하大亂(대란)의 시대에 태어나 山戰水戰(산전수전)을 다 거친 大人物(대인물)의 폭과 깊이를 드러낸다. 죽음을 앞두고도, 전쟁으로 고생한 백성들을 배려하는 마음이 뭉클하게 다가오는 名文이다. 민족사상 최대의 업

적을 남긴 인물이 죽음 앞에서 보여주고 있는 인생無常(무상)의 겸허함!

세속오계를 잇는 人性敎育 五戒

眞際 대선사는 이 책에서 人性敎育 五戒를 소개한다.

첫째는 국가와 사회에 필요한 사람이 됩시다.

둘째는 부모와 조상님께 효도합시다.

셋째는 친구와 이웃을 사귐에 있어 서로 信義(신의)와 사랑으로 합시다.

넷째는 맡은 바 일에 있어 성실과 정성을 다합시다.

다섯째는 大慈悲心을 가지고 뭇 생명을 존중합시다.

이 가르침은 1,400여 년 전 원광법사가 쓴 세속오계의 맥을 이었음을 알 수 있다.

1. 事君以忠(사군이충): 나라를 섬김에 충성을 다하라.
2. 事親以孝(사친이효): 부모를 섬김에 효성을 다하라.
3. 交友以信(교우이신): 벗을 사귐에 믿음으로 하라.
4. 臨戰無退(임전무퇴): 전쟁에 나가서는 물러나지 말라.
5. 殺生有擇(살생유택): 살아있는 것을 죽일 때는 가려서 하라.

'참나'의 自覺은 통일의지로 승화된다

신라의 삼국통일을 이끈 힘은 '참나'를 발견한 집단의 무서운 정신력인데 未堂 徐廷柱(미당 서정주) 시인은 문학적 통찰력으로 이를 정리하였다. 그는, 6·25 사변 때 하도 참혹한 것을 많이 보고 당한 뒤 자살까지 생각하는 지경에 몰렸다가 신라정신을 통하여 구원을 받았고, 그 뒤 신라정신을 詩作(시작)의 한 주제로 삼았음을 고백한 적이 있다.

"6·25 전쟁 중 극심한 절망감 속에서 나는 '國難(국난)이 닥쳤을 때 우리 옛 어른들 가운데 그래도 제 정신 차려 살던 이들은 난국을 무슨 슬기와 용기와 실천력으로 헤쳐 왔던가?' 하는 것을 절실히 알아보고 싶은 생각이 들어 마음속으로 더듬거려 보던 끝에 요체는 멀리 보고 한정 없이 언제까지나 끝없이 가려는 영원성이다.

"인생행로를 제한받고 또 스스로도 제한하며 얼마만큼만 가고 말려는 한정된 단거리주의가 아니라 한정 없이 언제까지나 가고 또 가려는 저 無遠不至(무원부지)주의, 신라인들에게서 우린 그걸 배워야 해. 그러면 불안과 불신과 반감과 충돌 따위를 훨씬 줄일 수 있겠지. 이 天地(천지)에 대한 주인의식이 신라인들에게 작용해 통일로 이끌어간 거지. 하늘과 땅을 맡아 생활하는 주인으로서 강한 책임의식. 이 점이 조선시대 유교가 우리민족에게 弱者(약자)의 팔자와 분수에 다소곳할 걸 가르쳐서 亡國(망국)의 길로 유도한 것과 전혀 다른 점이지. 각 개인의 값이나 민족의 가치는 에누리 당하자면 한정이 없고, 에누리만 해나가다가는 민족의 장래가 정말 암담할 수밖에 없는 거야. 나와 내 민족의 존엄성은 스스로 지킬 줄 알아야지. 하늘과 땅과 역사의 주인 된 자로서 말이네."

徐廷柱가 말한 '이 天地에 대한 주인의식'이야말로 眞際 대선사가 이 책에서 거듭 강조하는 '참나'의 정신인 것이다. '참나'의 自覺은 한반도의 현실을 직시할 때 필연적으로 통일의지로 승화할 수밖에 없다.

한반도의 자유, 동북아의 번영, 세계의 평화

진제 大禪師가 지도하는 한국의 불교계는 2015년 광화문 대집회를 통해 '민족통일'을 한국불교와 참선 수행의 話頭로 공표하였다. 민족통일의 핵심은 핵무기 발사 단추를 만지작거리는 젊은 독재자에 눌려 짐승처럼, 노예처럼 살고 있는 2,500만 衆生의 구원이다. '참나'를 발견한 불교인들이 그 자각을 행동으로 옮긴다면 가능한 일이다. 이 책은 한국불교에 분명한 목적의식을 설정하고 그 해결책까지 제시하고 있다.

"모든 煩惱妄想(번뇌망상)을 놓아버리고 참나를 깨달아 세상의 주인이 되면 언제 어디서나 걸림 없는 大自在의 삶을 살게 됩니다."

운명·역사·우주의 주인만이 누릴 수 있는 自由自在의 삶을 노래한 《참선이란 무엇인가?》한반도의 자유, 동북아의 번영, 세계의 평화를 구현하는 데 '眞際', 즉 '진실의 순간(Moment of truth)'을 가져오기를 기원한다.

Foreword

Cho Gab Je
CEO of chogabje.com

Seon Master Jinje's Book Declares the Revival of Buddhism

The Future Path of Buddhism: Unification of Korea and Seon Practice

Body of God

It was a snowy winter day a few years ago. Someone came and told me that Seon Master Jinje wished to see me, so I travelled down to Daegu city to hear his discourse and converse with him. Naturally he emphasized the importance of Seon practice, but, what impressed me even more than his question, "Why don't you pretend as if you were not born at all and study the way?" was the way he carried himself.

His composed and graceful demeanor made me think of the word *Wongongshinche*. The Sacred Bell of King Seongdeok the Great (also known as the Bongdeoksajong), which is housed in the Gyeongju National Museum, is also popularly referred to as the Emille Bell. It has 640 praises carved on it which carry forth the word Wongongshinche. This is not just another bell. Its massive globe-like figure and hollow interior is said to symbolize the 'Body of God.'

The fact that the attributes of God are thought to be circular and empty has a profound meaning. Imagine a regal-looking person without much ego who radiates calm and simplicity. Such a person evokes thoughts of the Buddha. They never quarrel with others, and because they have emptied themselves of all ego, they acknowledge the conflicts and wishes of all, to come together in a perfect harmony.

After reading the book What is Seon?, I came to realize that Master Jinje is just such a person, and that through the practice of Ganhwa Seon anyone can attain this level of realization.

The Moment of Truth

Since my life's work is writing, I've always been interested in names and titles. After meeting Master Jinje, I thought about the name "Jinje" and what it truly meant. I was able to find the answer after reading this book.

"Master Hyanggok was overjoyed and said, 'That's right, that's right!' Master Hyanggok then entrusted me with the

Dharma lamp of the Linji lineage, gave me the new Dharma name Jinje, and bestowed on me a Dharma Transmission Verse. It was 1967 and I was 33 years old."

"Jin" means "truth" and "je" means "time or moment." Thus, Jinje means "the time of truth." Actually, "je" does not refer to a particular time or moment; it has more the meaning of "close to." Therefore, "close to the moment of realizing the truth" in short will be "the moment of truth."

English has the term "moment of truth." This in fact best describes what the name Jinje truly means. The moment of truth is often translated into "a significant moment." The moment a man realizes the truth has great significance, and that moment becomes a historic moment in time. For Buddhists this can be described as "The moment of Realization."

Jinje! What a great name. He upholds the lineage of "Ganhwa Seon" passed down from the Buddha and all the past patriarchs, so there is no other name more appropriate for such a great master. According to his book, Ganhwa Seon is the only traditional Buddhist lineage that still exists.

The Way for an Ordinary Person to Become a Great Buddha
Born in Namhae, Gyeongsangnam-do province, Master Jinje

recalls that meeting Seon Master Seogu Bohwa at Haegwan-am Hermitage was the moment that changed his life.

When Master Seogu saw this mountain monk (Jinje), he immediately said, "Secular life is good, but there is an even worthier life. Would you like to give it a try?"

Master Jinje then asked, "What is this life you regard much worthier?"

Seogu responded, "There is a way that makes an ordinary person become a great Buddha. Why don't you pretend that you have not been born at all in this life and devote it wholly to seeking this marvelous way?"

Master Jinje accepted and began his monastic life, ultimately attaining great realization; he was awakened to his "true self." Then what is this "true self" he found? The book focuses on this particular point.

"Awakening to your true self means to awaken to the master within. I ask each of you, 'What is it that is sitting here listening to me speak right now?' When you awaken to this master within, it will become the master of everywhere, living a free life without hindrance.

By not relying on anything but this unchangeable true self, you will be liberated from all religious, political, and cultural restraints and live harmoniously with all beings. Awakening to our true self is the hope of the human race from which the future will unfold... Such integrity, happiness, freedom, and impartiality cannot be obtained merely through education or wealth, how devoutly you live your life, or through your position or sterling reputation. Rather, only a person who has awakened to their true self can be so blessed.

At the moment of death, with a clear mind and bright spirit, you will let go of this physical body, just as if you are changing clothes, and in the next life you will definitely attain great awakening.

However, if you neglect Seon practice, you will waste your life in discriminations, disputes, and conflicts, resulting in suffering and remorse. On your deathbed, it will be too late to have regrets about how you wasted your life."

One who has awakened to their true self is independent and unstoppable, a person of great freedom. That person is also a Buddha.

Master Jinje also describes the path to enlightenment through various parables.

"Then what is the most crucial part of Seon practice? If you are given a *hwadu*, keep to your own, but if you do not have a *hwadu*, use "What is your true self before you are born of your parents?" Hold this *hwadu* most fervently and ardently focus on it in your daily life until an unceasing doubt is generated and your single-minded focus on the *hwadu* flows."

From Gwanghwamun Plaza

The following is an excerpt from the dharma talk given by Master Jinje on May 16, 2015 at the Great Equality Assembly of Ganhwa Seon and Conference for World Peace and Reunification Korea in celebration of the 70th anniversary of Korean independence.

"If you immediately let go of all delusions, you reclaim your original ground of the mind as well as your true nature. Deluded, you are a sentient being, but illuminated, you are a Buddha. An ordinary man is no different from a sage in his original ground of the mind; he is light, life, peace and great freedom.

Hence, whoever has awakened to their true self can enjoy eternal happiness and great wisdom. Therefore, it is said that mind is Buddha and a person is also a Buddha. We should all make a vow to realize that all people are Buddhas, to respect each other and to live in harmony. An old sage once said, 'Be your own master wherever you are, and you will immediately be your own truth.' When you let go of your mental afflictions and delusions and become your own master by attaining your true self, you will live a life of great unhindered freedom wherever you are."

In realizing your "true self" you can lead a life of freedom without any hesitation and become the owner of natural phenomenon, the holder of your own destiny, of your own history, and the entire universe.

That is the true meaning of human freedom. The path of meditation is in fact a lonely and isolated path, but can bring victory and lead to the salvation of mankind.

Korean Buddhism and Reunification

On the day I first met Master Jinje, that snowy winter day a few years ago, I received a *hwadu* on reunification of the Korean Peninsula, and I made a wish for Korean Buddhism to become a patriotic Buddhism as it once was in Silla.

Last year in Gwanghwamun Plaza during the "2015 Buddhist Declaration for Peace on the Korean Peninsula", hundreds of thousands of Buddhists gathered and declared that Buddhism must play a pivotal role in reuniting North and South Korea.

Seon Master Jinje emphasized, "All defilements will dissipate from our mind when we incorporate our practice in daily life. Thus, I am certain that if we plant this seed in the minds of all Korean people, all jealousy, envy, and conflict will disappear. Thus, the unification of North and South Korea will be realized that much sooner."

Thus, the reunification of Korea was chosen as a *hwadu* for Korean Buddhism. Master Jinje then explained the path to reunification from the Buddhist perspective. For both North and South Koreans, the effort to attain our "true selves" is essential in overcoming conflict and division. This will help us reach the home of the mind where we will bask forever in great freedom, wisdom and peace.

The best historical achievement of Korean Buddhism was the unification of the Three Kingdoms.

Master Wongwang proposed a code of discipline for the laity (and the militants), which became the basic principles of the *Hwarangdo*. Master Wonhyo accomplished the reconciliation of different Buddhist schools; Master Euisang attempted to overcome the aftermath of war through the Flower Garland Sect in Korea.

There were also many others who worked with the *Hwarangdo*, including Chunchu Kim, Yooshin Kim, and Bubmin Kim. Buddhist philosophy and its worldview were the protagonist in unifying Korea's Three Kingdoms, and with the Korean Peninsula as their primary base, a new nation was created which eventually became the Republic of Korea.

When religion and relations between the kingdoms became entangled, the nation, the people, and religion, which was the foundation of them all, suffered. But during the Silla period, the government and Buddhism coexisted to secure the nation's independence. Now 1,300 years later, great Seon Master Jinje once again revealed the direction Korean Buddhism must take (toward reunification) and what people should work toward (finding one's true self). This is also the way to revive Buddhism.

Baekje and Goguryeo were both defeated by Tang China, the most powerful empire at that time. Tang then went further to place Silla under its rule. But Silla stayed autonomous for seven years, until its final stages. Silla was composed of communities that knew their "true self." In fact, one of the most eminent figures in Buddhism and in the fight for independence was General Yushin Kim.

Busik Kim of Goryeo described Yooshin Kim in History of the Three Kingdoms or the *Samguksagi* (삼국사기, 三國史記). He said Yooshin Kim was the embodiment of independence and the most important figure in the Three Kingdoms period (the author's descriptions of the general is more detailed than that of any king).

In 660 A.D. when Baekje was defeated by Nadang allies and Tang Gen. So Dingfang tried to destroy Silla, Yushin Kim argued as follows:

"A dog fears his master, but when the master steps on its feet, the dog will attack. Then, how can we not retaliate when we are faced with such a crisis?"

When Silla was preparing for battle, Tang Gen. So Dingfang breaks the attack of Silla and reported to Emperor Gaozong. The emperor asked, "Why not take Silla too, while you are at it?"

Busik Kim answered, "Silla has a wise emperor who loves his people. His subjects are loyal in serving their country, and the young respect their elders. Although the nation may be small, we cannot be careless and attack."

That was high praise to Silla from an enemy general. In other words, Silla was a nation where the king, his people and his subjects united to remain independent. Such coherence was only possible with the spirit of Buddhism.

Note the remark Gen. So Dingfang made. He stated, "The subjects are loyal to their country" rather than "The subjects are loyal to the king." This implies that the state was more important than the king. Placing more importance on the state rather than the king was seen not only in the orient but also during the French Revolution in the 18th century. The people of Silla placed the nation higher than the king. Perhaps this amazing perspective also displays the general values of Buddhism.

Thoughts on Killing

Ven. Wongwang composed five precepts for the laity during the reign of Silla's King Jinpyeong. Ven. Wongwang also sent a letter requesting assistance from the Sui dynasty. Although it was not appropriate conduct for a Buddhist monk, Buddhism ultimately received great praise for protecting the nation from collapse. The following response to Sui was recorded by Ven. Wongwang at the request of King Jinpyeong: "Though destroying others for one's own survival is not befitting for a monk, I live in your majesty's land and eat and drink what belongs to you. How dare I disobey your orders?" And so the beautiful Buddhist culture even seeped into politics and war.

Ven. Wongwang's five lay precepts maintained a delicate balance between the Buddhist philosophy of not taking life and the "no retreat" mindset of the Silla's militants. In essence the precepts said that one should fight bravely for one's own country, but killing must be kept to a minimum. Such modern rationality was rare even in ancient times.

King Munmu's name reflects both the compassionate side of Buddhism and the bravery and persistence of the Hwarang philosophy. "Mun" represents an element of Buddhism such as that found in religion, art and architecture. King Munmu unified the Three Kingdoms, and this power was reflected in his name which integrated the Chinese characters "mun" and "mu."

As written in the History of the Three Kingdoms, King Munmu's last words on his deathbed were remarkable. It is said that they are unequaled in the history of humanity. His dying words give us a glimpse into the character of this brave king who gave up everything in the face of death. They are as follows:

"Peaks and valleys are bound to change, and the day for a new generations will dawn. There are no golden plated birds found in the grave of Sun Qian nor in the grave of Cao Cao, only the name of the bronze sparrow (銅雀) is heard. The heroes of yesterday also died and became only a handful of earth. An apprentice carpenter sings on top and the fox rabbit will dig a hole nearby. Wasting all resources, what is left for the record is only pointless slander. Only vain labors are left behind, and the soul of a person cannot be saved. In quiet reminiscing my heart cries out, 'This is not what I enjoy.' Within ten days after my death, cremate my body in the Indian tradition in the courtyard. Follow the proper procedures, but keep the funeral to a minimum. Unnecessary taxes and bills must be restrained accordingly, and erroneous laws and formalities must all be resolved if possible. Then declare all this to the public for all to see, and the officers must enforce what has been said."

King Munmu's last words were humane. It is obvious that he was born into a chaotic world and that his great character was molded by all the misery and turmoil he had seen and experienced. His last words were finely composed, showing his considerate nature as he worried about the people who had suffered in war even as he himself lay dying. For someone who had accomplished so much, he was truly humble in the face of death.

The Five Virtues and Five Precepts for the Laity

Master Jinje introduced five virtues of character development in this book.

First, make a positive contribution to society.

Second, honor your parents and respect your elders.

Third, be loyal and respectful to your friends, and be kind to your neighbors.

Fourth, be sincere and earnest in carrying out your responsibilities.

Fifth, respect all life with love and compassion.

This teaching follows the teachings of Master Wongwang from 1,400 years ago.

1. Be loyal in serving your country
2. Pay respect to your parents
3. Take friends in truth and faith
4. Do not retreat in war
5. Be discerning in whom you kill

Finding Your True Self and the Reunification of Korea

The power that unified the Three Kingdoms was a great communal spirit. The poet Jeongju Seo summarized this with literary insight. He had seen horrific things in the Korean War which made him suicidal. But he later confessed that he had been redeemed through the spirit of Silla and was able to begin anew. He said:

"I thought deeply on what wisdom, courage, and the practices our ancestors had to survive the hopelessness of war. I explored sincerely and found that it was about looking far and wide and having persistence."

"When the course of life is limited, and when you limit yourself, then what allows you to move forward is not short sightedness but wishing to move forward without limits. We must learn that from the people of Silla. Then, all anxiety, distrust, hate and conflict is reduced significantly. The people of Silla achieved unification with the spirit of mastering their universe. To live as a master who can lead heaven and earth, you need a great sense of responsibility. This is radically different from the teachings of Joseon era Confucianism which instructed people to live as subordinates. The future is bleak if the value of each individual and the worth of the nation are restrained. We must be able to respect ourselves and our people. We are the masters of heaven earth and of our own history."

The master of the universe, as referred to by the poet Jeongju, is in fact the essence of the "True Self" that Master Jinje often emphasizes in this book.

When we realize our true self, facing the reality of the current state of the Korean Peninsula will inevitably be channeled into a commitment for the reunification of Korea.

Freedom on the Korean Peninsula, the Prosperity of Northeast Asia, and World Peace

During the 2015 Gwanghwamun Assembly, Korean Buddhists, under the direction of Great Seon Master Jinje, established reunification of the Korean Peninsula as the *hwadu* for Seon practitioners and Korean Buddhism as a whole. At the very heart of national unification lies the salvation of 25 million Koreans who live in fear like animals or slaves due to the distress caused by the actions of a young dictator who threatens them with nuclear missiles. Reunification is possible if the Buddhists who have found their "True Self" put into practice what they have realized. This book establishes a clear sense of purpose for Korean Buddhism and also presents a path to reunification.

"Cast aside all defilements and illusions and awaken to your true self to become the master of the universe. You will then enjoy eternal freedom without any hindrances."

It is my wish that this book, which sings the songs of freedom only enjoyed by the masters of destiny, history and the universe, will bring freedom to the Korean Peninsula, prosperity to Northeast Asia, and ultimately peace to the world.

추천사

김홍신
소설가

종정이란 호칭만 떠올려도 두손 모으고 절로 조아리게 됩니다.

진제 종정 예하께서 천하를 둥둥 울리고 향기롭게 하는 법어를 내리시어 정법대궐을 꾸미시자 만물이 흠향하였으며 뭇 중생들 마음이 꽃처럼 피어나 참살이를 하게 되었습니다.

대선사께서는 우리시대 대지혜의 상징이자 선정의 정좌요, 걸림 없는 참자유의 선포자이며, 아슬아슬하게 살아가는 사람들에게는 보살행의 상징입니다.

진제 대선사의 법어는 어둠속에서 갈 길을 잃은 중생들에게 광채가 되며, 이 땅에 계시는 것만으로도 평화를 증득케 하였습니다.

주장자를 드시고 "어떤 것이 참나인가"라는 화두를 던지시면 어찌 우러러보며 간화선 수행을 게을리 할 수 있겠습니까. 이번 생에 태어나지 않은 셈치고 수행에 몰두하라는 가르침은 참나를 밝히는 청정한 본분입니다. 이렇듯 종정께서는 다겁다생에 지어온 모든 습기를 녹여 없애는 정법이 되어, 생사를 요달할 깨달음의 본질을 일러 주셨습니다.

생로병사 해탈의 경지에 드시고 대오견성의 깨달음에 드신 대선사께서는 "부모에게 나기 전에 어떤 것이 참나인가?"라는 화두를 초대종정 석우 선사께 받아 오직 일념으로, 스스로 몸을 낮추시어 산승이라 겸어하시며 너와 내가 다르지 않고 둘은 곧 하나라는 불이의 지혜를 주셨습니다.

이에 대선사의 가르침을 받은 중생들은 삿됨을 금하고 청정행으로 예하의 뜻을 받들 것입니다. 어찌 고담한 준론을 받들지 않을 수 있겠습니까?

불조의 심인법은 서역 인도의 석가모니 부처님으로부터 마하가섭으로 전해져 제 28조 달마대사까지 면면히 이어진 후 중국을 거쳐 한국, 일본, 베트남 등으로 전해졌습니다.

지금은 인도는 물론 중국, 일본에도 정통 심인법은 소멸되고 오롯이 우리나라에만 남아 있습니다. 이 정통 심인법은 고려 때에 태고보우 국사로부터 근대에는 경허선사로 전승되고 불조심인 제 79대 법손인 진제종정께 이르렀습니다.

그럼에도 진제 대선사는 푸근하고 자상하고 웃어주고 쓰다듬어 주시는 참으로 곱게 나이 드신 산골 이웃집 할아버지 같습니다.

대선사께서 지혜의 등불을 높이 들어 마음 속 세 가지 어둠인 욕심, 화냄, 어리석음을 몰아내고 참 공덕으로 자비로운 마음과 풍요로운 세상을 꿈꾸게 해주시길 간청합니다. 그리하여 우리 모두 괴로움 없이 자유로운 사람이 되어 이 땅이 정토세상이 되도록 보살도를 펼쳐주소서.

공경하고 찬탄합니다.
부지런히 정진하겠습니다.
이생의 불법인연 하늘보다 높습니다.

두손 모아

Introduction

Kim Hong Sin
Writer

The title "supreme patriarch" leads one to feel great respect and wanting to bow with both palms together.

Supreme Patriarch Jinje teaches like he is decorating the dharma palace with his dharma teachings, with the sounds of profound dharma drums and fragrant flowers everywhere. The universe rejoices and the minds of sentient beings blossom in happiness.

Seon Master Jinje is an icon of our times who demonstrates true wisdom and who lives in freedom without any afflictions or defilements. He is a true Bodhisattva for people like us who live in this challenging world.

For those who are lost in the darkness, his teachings lead them to radiant light, and he brings peace just by remaining on this earth.

He holds out the dharma staff and teaches the *hwadu*, "What is your true self?" How can we not look up to him in awe and continue our practice with diligence?

Master Jinje teaches us to dedicate this life to understanding who we truly are and to indulge in spiritual practice as if we had never been born at all. Thus, seek out the dharma as your spiritual friend, and it will dissolve all your bad karma from eons of lives. It will help you understand the true meaning of life and death, and will lead you toward great enlightenment.

Master Jinje first received the *hwadu*, "What was your true self before you were born of your parents?" from Great Master Seogu, the first Supreme Patriarch of the Jogye Order. He fervently holds this *hwadu* with single-pointed concentration and calls himself a simple mountain monk. He teaches the non-duality of Buddhist wisdom and helps us understand that you and I are not separate but all are one and the same.

All sentient beings who receive teachings from Master Jinje will refrain from defilements and live by the teachings performing pure actions. How can we ignore what he has taught us?

The "mind-to-mind seal of Dharma" was transmitted from Sakyamuni Buddha to Mahākāśyapa, and continued on to the 28th patriarch, Bodhidharma, who introduced it to China. It was later introduced to Korea, Japan and Vietnam.

The Sixth Patriarch Huineng returned to the fundamental spirit of Buddhism, which was to attain enlightenment and liberation from birth and death. He established Patriarchal Seon, a path to sudden enlightenment by seeing one's true nature. Later, the Seon tradition of the Five Houses ushered in the golden era of Seon, which first spread throughout China and later was introduced to Korea and Japan.

However, in spite of this long history, the "mind-seal of Dharma" disappeared from India, China and Japan, and now only remains in its pure form in Korea. Master Taego Bou of the Goryeo era taught it to Master Gyeongheo, and now Master Jinje transmits this orthodox Seon lineage of Korean Buddhism as the 79th lineage holder.

Despite his lofty status, Seon Master Jinje still acts as if he is an elder from our neighborhood. He lives well, and he is now caring and laughing with us just like a grandfather figure often seen in the countryside.

My prayers go out to the master to teach the great lamp of wisdom which will eliminate the three darknesses from our minds (anger, greed, and ignorance), and may his compassion remake this world anew and prosperous. Let us be freed from suffering and let all live as if we are in the Pure Land.

With great reverence and admiration,

I promise to practice with diligence.

Thank you for creating a connection to the Buddha-Dharma in this life, that which is higher than heaven.

With palms together

차 례

추천사   東堂 성낙인 (서울대학교 총장) ·· 18
         조갑제 (조갑제닷컴 대표) ··· 27
         김홍신 (소설가) ··· 57

1   진제 대선사의 오도송(悟道頌) ·· 66
2   진영찬(眞影讚) ·· 68
3   대한불교조계종 종정 진제 대선사 약력 ··· 76
4   세계 간화선 무차대법회 상당법어 ··· 80
5   광화문 울린 종정 스님의 선문답(禪問答) 2015. 5. 20. 〈조선일보〉 김한수 기자 ··············· 107
6   30만 사부대중 한반도 통일, 세계 평화 위해 합장 2015. 5. 20. 〈중앙일보〉 배은나 객원기자 ····· 121
7   대한불교조계종 종정 진제 스님 한반도 통일을 꿈꾸다 2015. 5. 18. 〈CNN〉 캐시 노벡 기자 · 129
8   덕산탁발화 암두밀계기의(德山托鉢話 巖頭密啓其意) ··· 137
9   조주 선사와 황벽 선사, 임제 선사의 거량(擧揚) ································· 154
10 불조심인전등 다례대재 법어(佛祖心印傳燈 茶禮大齋 法語) ····························· 168
11 덕산 스님의 깨달음 ··· 178
12 간화선, 최상승(最上乘)의 경절문(徑截門) ·· 194
13 세계 평화를 위한 간화선 대법회 상당법어 ·· 243
14 UN 세계종교지도자모임 초청법회 법어 ·· 281
15 인성교육 오계(人性敎育 五戒) ·· 301
16 전법(傳法)의 원류(源流) ··· 313
17 간화선 수행법(看話禪 修行法) ··· 344

CONTENTS

Preface	Sung Nak In (Chancellor of Seoul National University)	22
Foreword	Cho Gab Je (CEO of chogabje.com)	40
Introduction	Kim Hong Sin (Writer)	60

1 Songs of Enlightenment by Seon Master Jinje 66

2 Eulogies Offered to Portraits of Great Korean Seon Masters 68

3 Profile of Seon Master Jinje Beopwon, the Supreme Patriarch 78

4 Dharma Talk at the Great Equality Assembly of Ganhwa Seon 93

5 Teaching by Master Jinje Echoes through Gwanghwamun Plaza
   〈Chosun Ilbo Report of 2015 Conference〉 112

6 Three Hundred Thousand Korean Buddhists Pray for World Peace and Reunification of Korea 〈Jooang Ilbo Report of 2015 Conference〉 124

7 Reunification is a Dream for South Korea's Buddhist Patriarch
   〈CNN Report of 2015 Conference〉 132

8 Deshan Carrying His Bowls 145

9 Dialogue between Zhaozhou, Huangbo and Linji 162

10 A Dharma Talk at the Great Memorial Ceremony for Buddhas and Patriarchs 173

11 Deshan's Awakening 186

12 Ganhwa Seon, the Supreme Path to Enlightenment 217

13 World Peace through Ganhwa Seon 261

14 World Peace and the Ecological Crisis: Buddhist Wisdom 291

15 The Five Virtues Leading to Character Development 307

16 Lineage of Seon Transmission 329

17 The Way of Ganhwa Seon 346

진제 대선사의 오도송 悟道頌
Songs of Enlightenment by Seon Master Jinje

이 주장자 이 진리를 몇 사람이나 알꼬?
과거, 현재, 미래의 모든 부처님도 다 알지 못함이로다.
한 막대기 주장자가 문득 금빛 용이 되어서
한량없는 용의 조화를 마음대로 부림이로다.

자개주장기인회 (這箇拄杖幾人會)아
삼세제불총불식 (三世諸佛總不識)이라.
일조주장화금룡 (一條拄杖化金龍)어니
응화무변임자재 (應化無邊任自在)로다.

How many people have known the truth of this Dharma staff?
None of the Buddhas of past, present or future do.
Suddenly this Dharma staff transforms into a golden dragon,
Performing innumerable wonders of the dragon entirely at will.

한 몽둥이 휘둘러 비로정상을 거꾸러뜨리고
벽력 같은 일 할로써 천만 갈등을 문대버림이로다.
두 칸 띠암자에 다리 펴고 누웠으니
바다 위 맑은 바람 만년토록 새롭도다.

일봉타도비로정 (一棒打倒毘盧頂)하고
일할말각천만측 (一喝抹却千萬則)이라.
이간모암신각와 (二間茅庵伸脚臥)하니
해상청풍만고신 (海上淸風萬古新)이로다.

One strike of this Seon staff, the peak of Mt. Biro collapses,

One thunderous roar crushes ten million Dharma teachings.

In this small thatched hut, I lie down stretching my legs.

A cool breeze over the ocean remains fresh for ten thousand years.

진영찬 眞影讚
Eulogies Offered to Portraits of Great Korean Seon Masters

1. 불조심인 제75조 경허 대선사 진영

　(佛祖心印 第七十五祖 鏡虛 大禪師 眞影)

사오백이 나열해 있는 화류항이요
이삼천이나 즐비한 관현루로다.
버드나무는 늘어져 나부끼고 저녁노을은 좋고 좋네
라라리리 남(生)이 없는 곡조로다.

사오백조화류항(四五百條花柳巷)이요
이삼천처관현루(二三千處管絃樓)라.
양류의의석양호(楊柳依依夕陽好)요
라라리리무생곡(囉囉哩哩無生曲)이로다.

〈문손 진제 분향찬(門孫 眞際 焚香讚)〉

To the portrait of Great Seon Master Gyeongheo,
the 75th Patriarch in the lineage of Sakyamuni Buddha

Four hundred, five hundred clubs dot the red-light district.
Two thousand, three thousand pavilions line the streets
Where lutes are played and zithers strummed.
Drooping willow branches billow and the sunset is glorious.
Lalala Lilili! These tunes have never come into being.

〈A eulogy and incense offered to Gyeongheo by the lineage holder Jinje〉

2. 불조심인 제76조 혜월 대선사 진영

(佛祖心印 第七十六祖 慧月 大禪師 眞影)

시냇물은 분주히 요란하게 흐르는데
백로는 한가로이 노니네.
일없는 老師(노사)는 솔방울 주워 메고
홀연히 이 몸 벗고 가시니 위없는 대열반이로다.

〈문손 진제 분향찬(門孫 眞際 焚香讚)〉

To the portrait of Great Seon Master Hyewol,
the 76th Patriarch in the lineage of Sakyamuni Buddha

The stream runs busily and boisterously
While a white crane plays leisurely.
The idle old master shoulders a bag of pine cones.
Suddenly he sheds his body, attaining unsurpassed nirvana.

〈A eulogy and incense offered to Hyewol by the lineage holder Jinje〉

3. 불조심인 제77조 운봉 대선사 진영

　(佛祖心印 第七十七祖 雲峰 大禪師 眞影)

저 건너 갈미봉에 비가 묻어오는데
우장 삿갓을 둘러쓰고 풍년가를 부르면서 논에 김을 매러 갈거나.
道를 道라 하면 道가 아닐세.

〈문손 진제 분향찬(門孫 眞際 焚香讚)〉

To the portrait of Great Seon Master Unbong,
the 77th Patriarch in the lineage of Sakyamuni Buddha

Rain begins to fall on the far side of Galmi Peak.
Shall I don a raincoat and bamboo hat, and go weed the rice paddy,
Singing songs of good harvest?
The way that can be named is not the Way.

〈A eulogy and incense offered to Unbong by the lineage holder Jinje〉

4. 불조심인 제78조 향곡 대선사 진영
   (佛祖心印 第七十八祖 香谷 大禪師 眞影)

봉암사의 큰 웃음 천년토록 기쁨이요
희양산의 굽이굽이 흐르는 물은 만년토록 한가롭네.
불법의 일구를 깨달으면 백억 년을 뛰어넘음이요
죽이고 살리는 자재의 수완을 갖춘 이가 몇몇이나 될고.

봉암대소천고희(鳳岩大笑千古喜)요
희양수곡만겁한(曦陽數曲萬劫閑)이로다.
일구요연초백억(一句了然超百億)이요
살활자재능기기(殺活自在能幾幾)이냐.

〈문하 진제 분향찬(門下 眞際 焚香讚)〉

To the portrait of Great Seon Master Hyanggok,
the 78th Patriarch in the lineage of Sakyamuni Buddha

A hearty laugh echoing inside Bongam-sa Temple is a joy
For a thousand years.
The meandering stream on Mt. Huiyang is idle
For ten thousand years.
Awakened to a single phrase of the Buddha-dharma,
One transcends ten billion years.
How many have attained the masterly skills of giving and taking
Life in total freedom?

〈A eulogy and incense offered to Hyanggok by the lineage holder Jinje〉

대한불교조계종 종정 진제 대선사 약력

1934년	경남 남해에서 출생
1953년	해인사에서 출가, 석우 스님을 은사로 사미계 수지
1957년	통도사에서 자운 스님을 계사로 구족계 수지
1959년	향곡 선사 문하에 입실, 간화선 수행
1967년	향곡 선사로부터 법을 인가받아, 경허-혜월-운봉-향곡 선사로 전해 내려온 정통법맥을 이음. 석가여래부촉법 제79대 법손
1971년	해운정사 창건
1979년	해운정사 금모선원 조실 (現)
1991년	선학원 이사장, 중앙선원 조실 역임
1994년	팔공산 동화사 금당선원 조실 (~2013년)
1996년	대한불교조계종 기본선원 조실 역임 (~2011년)
1998년	백양사 1차 무차선대법회 초청법주
2000년	백양사 2차 무차선대법회 초청법주
	조계종 종립 봉암사 태고선원 조실 역임
2002년	해운정사 국제무차선대법회 법주
2003년	대한불교조계종 원로의원
2004년	대한불교조계종 대종사 (現)

2009년	부산 벡스코 백고좌대법회 법주
2011년	미국 뉴욕 리버사이드 교회 간화선대법회 법주
2012년	미국 국가조찬기도회 60주년 행사 법문
	대한불교조계종 제13대 종정 (現)
	UN 세계종교지도자 초청법회
2013년	대한불교조계종 간화선대법회 법주 법문
	팔공총림 동화사 초대 방장 승좌 (現)
2015년	광복 70주년 한반도 통일과 세계 평화를 위한 세계 간화선 무차대법회 법주

법어집

《돌사람 크게 웃네(石人大笑)》, 《禪 백문백답》, 《염화인천(拈華人天)》
《고담녹월(古潭漉月)》, 《石人은 물을 긷고 木女는 꽃을 따네》 등

영문 법어집

《Open the Mind, See the Light》
《Finding the True Self》 등

Profile of Seon Master Jinje Beopwon, The Supreme Patriarch

1934	Born in Namhae, South Gyeongsang-do Province, Republic of Korea
1953	Entered Haein-sa Monastery, received novice ordination from Seon Master Seogu
1957	Received full Bhikkhu ordination at Tongdo-sa Monastery
1959	Began practice under guidance of Seon Master Hyanggok
1967	Received Dharma transmission from Master Hyanggok, continuing the lineage of Masters Gyeongheo, Hyewol, Unbong, and Hyanggok. Recognized in Korea as the 79th Patriarch in the Dharma lineage originating with Sakyamuni Buddha.
1971	Founded Haeunjeong-sa Temple in Busan
1979	Installed as Josil (Guiding Seon Master) of Geummo Seon Hall at Haeunjeong-sa
1991	Appointed Chairman of the Board, Institute of Seon Studies. Appointed Guiding Master of Central Seon Center
1994	Appointed Josil of Donghwa-sa Monastery (~2013)
1996	Appointed Josil of the "Fundamental Seon Practice," responsible for overseeing the Seon training of monks in the Jogye Order of Korean Buddhism (~2013)
1998	Invited to be a presiding Seon Master for the First Equal Assembly of Seon, held at Baekyang-sa Monastery
2000	Invited to be a presiding Seon Master for the Second Equal Assembly of Seon, held at Baekyang-sa
	Invited to be Josil of Taego Seon Hall at Bongam-sa Monastery
2002	Presiding Seon Master of the International Great Equal Assembly of Seon, held at Haeunjeong-sa

2003	Joined a member of the Council of Elders, Jogye Order of Korean Buddhism
2004	Awarded the title of Daejongsa, "most eminent monk" by the Jogye Order of Korean Buddhism
2009	Appointed Presiding Seon Master of the "Hundred-Seat Dharma Assembly" held in the BEXCO center, Busan, South Korea
2011	Dharma Talk on "Ganhwa Seon and World Peace" at New York Riverside Church
2012	Attended the 60th National Prayer Breakfast in the US
	Dharma Talk for International Leadership Seminar
	Appointed Supreme Patriarch of the Jogye Order of Korean Buddhism
	Dharma Talk at UN Plaza on "World Peace and the Ecological Crisis;- A Buddhist Wisdom"
2013	Appointed Presiding Seon Master Great Assembly of Ganhwa Seon, held at Jogye-sa Temple
	Installed as Bangjang (Spiritual Master) of Dongwha-sa monastry
2015	Presiding Seon Master of the Great Equal Assembly of Ganhwa Seon, for the Conference for World Peace and Harmony

Publications

Korean 《The Stone Man Laughs》
《Seon, One Hundred Questions and Answers》
《Lotus of Man and Heaven》
《Moon Pulled Out from an Old Pond》
《A Stone Man Fetches Water, a Wooden Maiden Picks Flowers》

English 《Open the Mind, See the Light》
《Finding the True Self》

세계 간화선 무차대법회 상당법어

2015.5.16. 광화문 광장

세계 간화선 무차대법회에서 상당법어하시는 종정 예하

Supreme Patriarch of the Jogye Order of Korean Buddhism
at the Conference for World Peace and Reunification of Korea

[상당하시어 불자를 들어 대중에게 보이시고,]

옛 부처가 나기 전에 누가 우주의 주인공인고?
고요하고 고요해서 그 체성은 평안한지라.
온 세계가 한 집이요
정이 있고 정이 없는 모든 만물이 한 몸이로다.

고불미생시수주(古佛未生是誰主)오
요요적적체평안(寥寥寂寂體平安)이라.
대천세계공일가(大千世界共一家)요,
정여무정동일체(情與無情同一體)로다.

대중 여러분께서는, 방금 산승이 말한 그 주인공을 아시겠습니까? 이 주인공은 천지만물(天地萬物)의 근본이요, 일체중생의 마음 자리입니다. 이 근본자리는 텅 비어 고요함이나 분명하고 분명한 자리입니다.

온갖 망령(妄靈)된 생각들을 즉각 내려놓는다면, 바로 그 자리가 본래의 마음자리며 본래의 참모습인 것입니다. 미혹(迷惑)하면 중생이요, 항상 밝아 있으면 부처이기에, 범부(凡夫)와 성인(聖人)이 근본 자리에서는 둘이 아님이요, 그대로 광명(光明)이요, 생명이요, 평화요, 대자유(大自由)입니다. 그렇기에 누구든지 참나를 깨달으면 영원한 행복과 대지혜(大智慧)를 누릴 수 있는 것입니다.

그러므로 마음이 곧 부처요, 사람이 곧 부처라고 말하는 것입니다. 이렇게 사람이 곧 부처임을 깨달아서 서로 존중하고 상생(相生)하는 삶을 만드는 일이 이 자리에 있는 우리가 이루어야 할 서원입니다.

옛 성인이 말씀하시기를 '가는 곳마다 주인이 되면, 서 있는 그 자리가 모두 진리의 세계'라고 했습니다. 모든 번뇌망상(煩惱妄想)을 놓아버리고 참나를 깨달아 세상의 주인이 되면 언제 어디서나 걸림 없는 대자재의 삶을 살게 됩니다.

번뇌에 미혹할 때는 고해(苦海)의 사바세계가 있으나, 참나를 깨달으면 시방이 공(空)하여 고통스러운 현실에서 곧바로 해탈열반(解脫涅槃)의 삶을 실현하는 지름길이 되는 것입니다.
부처님께서는 자비의 원력으로 중생을 위해 겨자씨만한 땅에도 피를 흘리지 않은 곳이 없다고 하셨으니 "중생이 아프니 나도 아프다"는 유마거사의 말씀이 오늘날 이 지구촌 인류에게 장군죽비가 되어야 할 것입니다.
모든 잘못을 남의 탓으로만 돌리고, 나 혼자만 구원받으면 된다는 오늘의 사회풍조 속에서 인격도야의 실천행이 더욱 절실하다 할 것입니다.

그러면 이렇게 참나를 깨달아서 영원한 행복과 대지혜를 얻고자 하면 어떠한 자세를 갖추어야 하고 어떻게 나아가야 하는지 산승이 만인에게 여섯 가지의 나아갈 길을 말씀드리고자 합니다.

첫째는   보시(布施)로 만복과 덕행을 쌓아야 함이요,

둘째는   지계(持戒)로 청정하고 성실하여 품행을 단정히 해야 함이요,
셋째는   인욕(忍辱)으로 마음에 일어나는 온갖 분별심을 이겨내어 장애를 걷어 내는 것이요,
넷째는   정진(精進)으로 일체처일체시(一切處一切時)에 화두를 잘 참구해 중생의 미혹한 마음을 닦는 것이요,
다섯째는 선정(禪定)으로 그렇게 마음을 닦아 온갖 두려움을 없애 참된 평화를 얻는 것이요,
여섯째는 지혜(智慧)로 일체를 다 알아 무애자재한 삶을 누리는 것입니다.

이렇게 여섯 가지 나아갈 길을 지극한 마음으로 금쪽같이 받아 행(行)하시면 필경(畢竟)에는 진리를 깨닫게 될 뿐만 아니라, 대중의 화합과 행복한 정토사회를 이루게 될 것입니다.

그러므로 산승은 금일 이 무차법회의 자리를 빌려 지구촌의 참된 평화와 인류의 영원한 행복을 위해, 그리고 세계에서 유일한

분단국가인 대한민국의 평화통일을 위해서 화두참선으로 참나를 깨닫는 '간화선(看話禪)'이라는 마음 닦는 수행법을 제시하고자 합니다.

그러면 인류문화의 정수(精髓)인 간화선은 어떻게 닦는 것인가? 간화선의 생명은 화두를 챙겨 간절히 의심하는 것입니다.

그러니 일상생활하는 가운데 '부모에게 나기 전에 어떤 것이 참나인가?' 이 화두를 들고 일체처일체시에 가나 오나 앉으나 서나 챙기고 의심하여, 오로지 간절한 화두의심 한 생각에 푸욱 빠지도록 하루에도 천 번 만 번 반복해서 챙기고 의심해야 합니다.

그러던 중 문득 일념삼매에 들어서 크게 죽었다가 홀연히 살아나게 되면 마침내 마음의 고향에 이르러 대자유와 대지혜와 대안락(大安樂) 그리고 대평화(大平和)를 영원토록 누리게 되는 것입니다.

이처럼 참나를 깨닫는 그 속에 영원히 마르지 않는 복락(福樂)이 있는 것이니, 그 무엇보다도 우선되어야 할 지중(至重)하고도 지중한 가치입니다.

그러면 모든 분께 대오견성(大悟見性)의 희망을 드리고자, 간화선 참선수행을 잘해서 진리를 깨달아 그 살림살이를 자유자재로 쓰다 가신 옛 도인들의 일화(逸話)를 말씀드리겠습니다.

지금으로부터 90여 년 전, 근대 한국불교의 중흥조이셨던 경허 선사의 상수(上首) 제자인 혜월(慧月) 선사로부터 심인법(心印法)을 전해 받은 제 77대 조사인 운봉(雲峰) 선사라는 대도인이 계셨습니다.

운봉 선사는 법을 이은 뒤에도 제방 선원을 두루 다니시면서 한 철 한 철을 여법(如法)히 수행에 몰두했습니다.

한 번은 경기도 망월사에서 "30년 결사(結社)를 하자" 하여 제방에서 발심한 스님 40여 명이 모였습니다. 당시에 조실 스님으로는 용성(龍城) 선사를 모셨고, 선덕(禪德)으로는 훗날 조계종 초대 종정(宗正)을 지낸 석우(石友) 선사를 모셨습니다. 입승(立繩)은 운봉 선사께서 맡아 모든 대중이 밤낮으로 여법(如法)히 참선정진에 몰두하고 있었습니다.

하루는 법회(法會)가 있어 용성 조실 스님께서 법상(法床)에 오르셔서 법문하시기를,

"나의 참모습은 과거 현재 미래의 모든 부처님도 보지 못함이요, 대대로 내려오는 모든 도인 스님들도 보지 못하니, 여기에 모인 모든 대중은 어느 곳에서 나를 보려는고?"

하고 멋진 법문을 던지셨습니다. 그러니 아무도 답이 없는 가운데 운봉 선사께서 자리에서 일어나 답을 하였습니다.

"유리 독 속에 몸을 감췄습니다."

이렇게 멋진 답을 하니, 용성 선사께서는 아무런 말없이 법상에

서 내려와 조실방(祖室房)으로 돌아가셨습니다.

　이 대목을 가지고 40여 년 전에 산승의 스승이자, 운봉 선사의 법제자이신 향곡(香谷) 선사께서 산승에게 물으시기를,
"만약 진제 네가 당시의 용성 선사가 되었다면, 운봉 선사가 '유리독 속에 몸을 감췄다'고 답할 때에 무엇이라 점검하고 법상에서 내려가겠는고?"
　하시니 산승이 즉시 답하기를,
"사자가 멋진 답을 하셨습니다."
　하니, 향곡 선사께서 매우 기뻐하셨으니, 전광석화(電光石火)와 같은 바른 안목(眼目)을 갖춘다는 것은 천고(千古)에 쉬운 일이 아닌 것입니다.
　이처럼 법(法)에 대한 스승과 제자의 안목이 줄탁동시(啐啄同時)에 이루어질 때 점검과 인가가 원만히 이루어지는 것입니다.

　또 한국의 신라와 동시대인, 중국의 당나라에는 위대한 방 거사(龐居士) 도인(道人) 일가족이 있었습니다. 부처님 선법(禪法)이 유래한 후로, 세속 사람들 가운데에 방 거사를 능가할 만한 안목을 갖춘 사람은 드뭅니다.
　당시는 마조(馬祖) 선사, 석두(石頭) 선사 두 분이 쌍벽을 이루어 당나라 천지에 선법을 크게 선양하시던 때였는데, 신심 있고 용맹심 있는 스님들과 마을 신도들은 모두 두 분 도인을 친견하여 법문

을 듣고 지도를 받았습니다.

 하루는 방 거사가 큰 신심과 용기를 내어 석두 선사를 친견하러 가서 예(禮) 삼배(三拜)를 올리고 여쭙기를,
 "만 가지 진리의 법으로 더불어 벗 삼지 아니하는 자, 이 누구입니까?"
 하고 아주 고준(高峻)한 물음을 던졌습니다.
 그러자 석두 선사께서는 묻는 말이 떨어지자마자 방 거사의 입을 틀어막았습니다. 여기에서 방 거사는 홀연히 진리의 눈이 팔부(八部)가 열렸습니다.
 "선사님, 참으로 감사합니다."
 석두 선사께 큰절을 올려 하직인사를 하고는, 그 걸음으로 수백 리 길을 걸어서 마조 선사를 친견하러 갔습니다.
 마조 선사 처소에 이르러 예 삼배를 올리고 종전과 같이 여쭙기를
 "만 가지 진리의 법으로 더불어 벗 삼지 아니하는 자, 이 누구입니까?"
 하니, 마조 선사께서
 "그대가 큰 서강수(西江水) 강물을 다 마시고 오면 그대를 향해 일러 주리라."
 하시는 이 고준한 한 마디에 진리의 눈이 활짝 열리게 되었습니다.
 모든 부처님과 모든 조사 스님들과 동일한 진리의 안목이 열린 것입니다. 그리하여 마조 선사의 제자가 되었습니다.

방 거사는 그런 후로 집에 돌아와서 대대로 물려받은 가보와 재산을 전부 마을 사람들에게 흔연히 보시(布施)했습니다. 그리고 자신은 가족과 함께 개울가에 오두막집을 한 칸 지어놓고 산죽을 베어다가 쌀을 이는 조리를 만들어 팔아 생활하면서 온 가족이 참선 수행에 몰두하였습니다.

부인 보살과 딸이 하나 있었는데, 부인 보살도 참선 수행하여 대도를 이루고, 딸도 결혼하지 않고 참선 수행하여 마침내 온 가족이 진리의 최고 안목을 갖추게 되었습니다.

방 거사 일가족이 다 견성(見性)을 하여 이렇게 멋지게 생활한다는 소문이 당나라 천하에 분분하니, 많은 도인이 방문하였습니다.

하루는 단하천연(丹霞天然) 선사께서 방 거사를 찾아오셨는데, 마침 딸인 영조(靈照)가 사립 앞 우물에서 채소를 씻고 있으니 천연 선사께서 묻기를,

"방 거사 있느냐?"

하시니, 영조가 채소 씻던 동작을 멈추고 일어서서 가슴에 양손을 얹고 가만히 서 있었습니다.

천연 선사께서 즉시 그 뜻을 아시고는 다시 어떻게 나오는지 시험해 보기 위해서,

"방 거사 있느냐?"

하고 재차 물으시니, 영조가 가슴에 얹은 양손을 내리고는 채소 바구니를 머리에 이고 집 안으로 들어가 버렸습니다.

이에 천연 선사께서도 즉시 되돌아가셨습니다.

말이 없는 가운데 말이 분명하니, 이러한 문답을 바로 볼 줄 알아야 진리의 고준한 안목을 갖추게 되고 만 사람을 진리의 도에 인도하게 될 것입니다.

어느 날 방 거사가 가족과 함께 방에서 쉬고 있다가 불쑥
"어렵고 어려움이여, 높은 나무 위에 일백 석이나 되는 기름통의 기름을 펴는 것과 같구나"
하니, 방 거사 부인 보살이 그 말을 받아서
"쉽고 쉬움이여, 일백 가지 풀 끝이 모두 불법의 진리이구나."
하고 반대로 나왔습니다. 그러자 딸 영조가 석화전광(石火電光)으로 받아서,
"어렵지도 아니하고 쉽지도 아니함이여, 피곤하면 잠자고 목마르면 차를 마신다."
라고 말했습니다.

그러면 여기 모이신 모든 대중은 방 거사 일가족을 아시겠습니까?

방 거사가 "어렵고 어려움이여, 높은 나무 위에 일백 석이나 되는 기름통의 기름을 펴는 것과 같구나" 한 것은 어떠한 진리를 표현한 것이며, 방 거사 부인 보살이 말한 "쉽고 쉬움이여, 일백 가지

풀 끝이 모두 불법의 진리이구나" 한 것은 어떠한 진리를 표현한 것입니까? 또, 영조가 말한 "어렵지도 아니하고 쉽지도 아니함이여, 피곤하면 잠자고 목마르면 차를 마신다"는 어떠한 진리의 세계를 드러낸 것입니까?

이 세 마디에 모든 성인과 모든 도인께서 설하신 법문이 다 들어 있으니, 이것을 가려낼 줄 안다면 모든 성인과 모든 도인과 어깨를 나란히 하는 것이니, 산승이 주석(住席)하고 있는 팔공총림의 동화사 방장(方丈)자리를 물려줄 것입니다.

그러면 여기에 답을 하실 분 있습니까?

[잠시 후]

그러면 온 세계가 간화선의 향기에 흠뻑 젖어 안락(安樂)의 고향에 머물고 일체중생이 만복을 성취하기를 바라는 뜻에서, 금일 산승이 한쪽 팔을 걷어붙이고 이 방 거사 일가족의 심오한 법문을 점검하여, 모든 인류에게 진리의 법공양을 올리겠습니다.

만약 산승이, 방 거사 일가족이 한마디씩 할 때 그 자리에 있었더라면, 좋은 차를 다려서 한 잔씩 드렸을 것입니다.
그러면 이 차를 한 잔씩 드린 것은 법문을 잘해서 드린 것입니까? 아니면 잘못해서 드린 것입니까?

대중은 아시겠습니까?

[잠시 후]

우리 조국에서 산화(散華)하신 영령(英靈)들,
거년(去年) 세월호 참사로 희생되신 모든 영가(靈駕)분과 네팔 대지진 참사로 희생되신 모든 영가들, 인류의 행복과 평화를 위하여 희생되신 모든 영가께서도 삼독(三毒)의 애착과 집착을 다 내려놓고 부처님의 극락정토(極樂淨土)에서 대 안락을 누리시기를 바라는 뜻에서 진리의 한 마디를 선사하고자 하노니 잘 받아 가지시기 바랍니다.

내년에 다시 나뭇가지에 새 움이 자라서
봄바람에 어지러이 쉬지 못함이로다.

내년갱유신조재(來年更有新條在)하야
뇌란춘풍졸미휴(惱亂春風卒未休)로다.

금일 이곳 광화문 광장에 모이신 모든 분, 이 한 마디를 잘 간직하셔서 무한한 진리의 낙을 누리시기 바랍니다.

[주장자로 법상을 한 번 치고 하좌하시다.]

광화문 광장 법회전경

Great Equality Assembly of Ganhwa Seon at Gwanghwamun Plaza

Dharma Talk at the
Great Equality Assembly of Ganhwa Seon

May 16, 2015, Gwanghwamun Plaza, Seoul

Who was the master of the universe

Before an old Buddha was born?

In deep tranquility the essence is at peace.

The whole universe is of a single family.

All sentient and insentient beings are of the same essence.

Assembly in attendance!

Who is the "master" this mountain monk just spoke of?

This master is the foundation of all things in the universe, and the ground of the mind for all sentient beings. This original ground is inherently empty and filled with stillness, but has distinct clarity.

If you immediately let go of all delusions, you reclaim your original ground of the mind as well as your true nature. Deluded, you are a sentient being, but illuminated, you are a Buddha. Just as an ordinary man is no different from a sage in the original ground of the mind, he is light, life, peace and great freedom. Hence, whoever has awakened to the true self can enjoy eternal happiness and great wisdom.

Therefore, it is said that mind is Buddha and a person also a Buddha. To realize that a person is a Buddha and to respect and live a mutually sustainable life are the vows we must make today.

An old sage once said, "Be your own master wherever you are, and you will immediately be your own truth." When you let go of your mental afflictions and delusions, and become your own master by attaining your true self, you will live a life of great unhindered freedom wherever you are.

When you are deluded by your mental afflictions, you experience the suffering of the secular world. However, when you attain your true self, the ten directions are empty and open to you. Then you can swiftly transform painful reality and actualize a life of liberation.

In his great vow of compassion for all sentient beings, the Buddha said there was no place in the universe, even as tiny as a mustard seed, where he hadn't been willing to sacrifice his own life for the sake of sentient beings. The sage Vimalakīrti said, "All sentient beings are ill, therefore I am ill." These words should be a huge warning for present-day humanity. In today's society that tends to think the salvation of self is enough, and that all wrongs are the fault of others, the cultivation of character and the deeds of Vimalakīrti are examples for us all.

Then, if you want to attain your true self, and achieve eternal happiness and great wisdom, what should you do? What attitude should you take and how should you proceed? This mountain monk would like to tell you the six paths you should take.

First, with generosity you can accrue immeasurable good fortune and perform virtuous deeds.

Second, with ethics you can act purely and uprightly.

Third, with patience you can overcome all discriminatory thoughts that arise from within and lift the veil that hinders your vision.

Fourth, with joyous effort you should investigate your own *hwadu* ceaselessly and transform the deluded minds of other sentient beings.

Fifth, with meditative concentration you should cultivate your mind, remove all fear and attain true peace.

Sixth, with wisdom you should know all things and live a life of great freedom.

If you receive and practice these six paths with utmost sincerity, you will not only awaken to the truth eventually but also establish harmony and happiness in a pure society.

Today this mountain monk wants to take this occasion of the Great Equal Assembly and introduce to you all "Ganhwa Seon," a practice of mind cultivation to attain your true self, which is based on the investigation of a *hwadu*. I do this for the sake of attaining genuine peace in our global community, of attaining everlasting happiness for humanity, and of attaining the peaceful reunification of Korea, the only remaining divided country on Earth.

Then, how do you practice Ganhwa Seon, the essence of

human spirituality? In Ganhwa Seon you investigate a *hwadu*, and what's most important in this practice is to build up "fervent doubt" about your own *hwadu*.

Therefore, in your daily life, investigate the *hwadu*,

"What is your true self before you are born of your parents?"

Build up doubt about this *hwadu* ceaselessly, whether coming or going, standing or sitting. You should engage and return to this *hwadu* a thousand times or tens of thousands of times a day. Suddenly, you will find yourself immersed in one-pointed concentration and dwelling in a state akin to death. Then suddenly, you come back to life, arriving at your mind's true home. From then on you can enjoy great freedom, great wisdom, great comfort and great peace for all eternity. In this way, inexhaustible joy and blessings can be found in the awakening of one's true self, and this should be your foremost and only goal in life

In order to give you hope of attaining great enlightenment, I'd like to tell you a few stories about past sages who attained the truth through Ganhwa Seon and achieved a life of unhindered freedom.

About 90 years ago, there lived a great sage named Master

Unbong (雲峰性粹), the 77th Patriarch of the Korean Seon lineage. Master Unbong received the "Mind-Seal" of the Buddha from Master Hyewol (慧月), the head disciple of Master Gyeongheo, a great sage who helped revive Korean Buddhism. As a Dharma heir, Master Unbong visited Seon monasteries all over Korea and concentrated on Ganhwa Seon practice sincerely during every meditation retreat.

One day, some Seon practitioners decided to engage together in a "Thirty-Year Practice Movement." About 40 monks with great aspirations for enlightenment flocked to Mangwolsa Temple in Gyeonggi-do Province from all over Korea. They had Master Yongseong (龍城震鍾; 1864~1940) as their guiding teacher. Master Seogu (石友; 1875~1958), the 1st Supreme Patriarch of the Jogye Order was their senior meditator, and Master Unbong was their rector. They all practiced earnestly day and night.

One day there was a Dharma assembly and Temple Master Yongseong ascended the Dharma seat. He began his talk by asking, "Even all Buddhas from the past, present and future can not see my true face, nor can all the generations of sage monks.

Monks in this assembly! Where can you see my true face?"

Nobody answered until Master Unbong stood and replied, "It hid itself inside a glass pot."

Upon hearing this splendid answer, Yongseong immediately descended from the Dharma seat in silence and went back to his room.

More than 40 years ago, my teacher, Master Hyanggok, questioned this mountain monk about that incident. "If you had been Master Yongseong, what would you have said to Master Unbong when he responded, 'It hid itself inside a glass pot.'?"

So I immediately responded, "A lion gave its best roar."

To this my teacher was greatly overjoyed. It is extremely difficult to have the correct perspective that enables one to respond in an instant. In this way, when a master and disciple experience the opportune moment to communicate on the same level of Seon attainment, the evaluation and certification of enlightenment are properly accomplished.

In Tang China, during the same era as Korea's Silla Dynasty, Layman Pang (龐居士) had a family, and all in his family were sages. He was perhaps the greatest householder sage to ever have been born since the Seon teachings of Buddha emerged.

At that time, two eminent Seon masters, Mazu (馬祖) and Shitou (石頭), were propagating Seon Buddhism widely in Tang China. Courageous monks of great faith and lay practitioners alike flocked to them to receive training and guidance.

One day, drawing upon faith and courage from the depth of his heart, Layman Pang went to see Master Shitou. He offered three bows and asked this noble question: "Who is he that is not a companion to the ten thousand Dharmas of the truth?"

Upon hearing this, Master Shitou placed his hands on Layman Pang's mouth and silenced him. Layman Pang's mind suddenly expanded about 80 percent.

"Master, thank you so much!"

Layman Pang then prostrated himself before Master Shitou and then walked hundreds of miles to meet Master Mazu.

Upon arriving at the residence of Master Mazu, he offered three deep prostrations and asked again: "Who is he that is not a companion to the ten thousand Dharmas of the truth?"

Master Mazu answered, "I will tell you after you have swallowed the entire West River in one gulp."

At these marvelous words, Layman Pang's wisdom eye was fully opened. He gained the supreme wisdom eye, equal to all the Buddhas and Patriarchs, and Layman Pang became Master Mazu's disciple.

When Layman Pang returned home, he readily gave away all his wealth and treasures to his neighbors. Afterward, he and his family lived a simple life in a small thatched hut near a river, supporting themselves by making bamboo utensils with bamboo from the mountains. The whole family just concentrated on the practice of Seon. His wife practiced Seon and attained the great way, and his daughter Lingzhou never married, only practicing Seon. At last one day, the eyes of the whole family were opened to the supreme truth.

As the story of Layman Pang's family spread throughout Tang China, many practitioners and sages came to witness the whole family living a life of freedom.

One day, when Lingzhou was washing vegetables at the well in front of the gate, Master Danxia Tianran (丹霞天然) came to visit and inquired, "Is Layman Pang home?"

Lingzhou stopped washing vegetables, stood up, and placed her palms on her chest respectfully in silence.

The Master understood her meaning right away, but to test Lingzhou, he asked again,

"Is Layman Pang home?" She answered by putting her hands down, picked up the basket of vegetables and went inside.

Upon this, Master Tianran turned and left at once.

Words are loud and clear in the absence of speech. When our ears are attuned to such words, we attain the noble eye of truth, and then we can guide ten thousand people to the path of truth.

One day, Layman Pang was resting at home with his family. He suddenly mumbled to his wife, "Difficult and difficult! It is like smearing the top of a tall tree with a hundred gallons of oil." His wife retorted, "Easy and easy! The truth of the Buddha-Dharma is reflected on the tips of a hundred blades of grass."

Lingzhou interrupted in a flash and said, "It's neither difficult nor easy. When I'm thirsty, I drink tea. When I'm tired, I sleep."

Present Assembly! Do you now understand the beauty of Layman Pang's family?

Which truth did Layman Pang express when he said, "Difficult and difficult! It is like smearing the top of a tall tree with a hundred gallons of oil?" Which truth did his wife express when she retorted, "Easy and easy! The truth of the Buddha-Dharma is reflected on the tips of a hundred blades of grass?"

And which realm of truth did Lingzhou reveal when she said, "It's neither difficult nor easy. When I'm thirsty, I drink tea. When I'm tired, I sleep?"

These three passages contain the Dharma talks taught by all enlightened sages of the past. If you can distinguish them, you will not only join the ranks of all the enlightened sages, but I will also appoint you to be the Spiritual Patriarch of Donghwasa Temple, the home of Palgong Chongnim (Palgong Comprehensive Monastic Training Complex).

Is there anyone here who can answer my questions?

[After a few moments]

Now, in my hope that the whole world be steeped in the fragrance of Ganhwa Seon and dwell in its peaceful spiritual home, and with my hope that all living beings receive ten thousand blessings, this mountain monk will roll up his sleeves, examine the profound teachings of Layman Pang's family, and give an offering of Dharma to all of humanity.

If this mountain monk had been present when each member of Pang's family spoke their passage, I would have brewed good tea and offered a cup of tea to each of them.

Is my tea offering adequate praise for their well-presented Dharma talks or an insult?

Assembly in attendance! Do you understand what I have said?

[After a few moments]

Spirits of those who lost their lives on the Korean Peninsula!
Spirits of those who lost their lives in the Sewol Ferry disaster!
Spirits of those who lost their lives in the horrendous Nepal earthquakes!
Spirits of those who sacrificed their lives for the happiness and peace of humanity!

I would like to offer one last passage of truth in hopes that all the spirits mentioned above let go of their clinging and all attachments, and enjoy great peace in the blissful land of the Buddha.

Buds will sprout again on a new branch in the coming year.
In the midst of the disturbing spring winds, there is no rest.

Members of the assembly gathered here at Gwanghwamun Plaza today!
I hope you embrace this passage well and enjoy the boundless joy of the Truth!

[The Master hits the Dharma staff once and descends the Dharma Seat.]

광화문 광장 대법회 행사장 전경
광복 70주년 한반도 통일과 세계 평화를 위한 세계 간화선 무차대회

Seoul Gwanghwamun Plaza transforms into a dazzling plaza of illumination
filled with lotus lanterns to wish for peace and harmony
at the Conference for World Peace and Reunification of Korea.

광화문 울린 종정 스님의
선문답(禪問答)

2015. 5. 20 〈조선일보〉 **김한수** 기자

"짝, 짝, 짝"

지난 16일 저녁 8시 24분, 서울 광화문 광장. 죽비 소리가 세 번 울렸다.

그러자 일순 광화문 광장은 정적에 빠졌다. 대한민국의 심장, 평소엔 늘 자동차와 사람 물결이 이어지는 곳, 때로는 시위대와 경찰이 대치하는 갈등 현장인 이곳에 평화로운 고요가 흘렀다. 명상에 든 30만 명은 지그시 눈을 감고 마음의 소리에 귀를 기울였다.

이날 열린 '한반도 통일과 세계 평화를 위한 기원대회-세계 간화선 무차대회'의 하이라이트인 선정(禪定)에 드는 시간이었다.

이날 광화문 광장은 평화와 지혜를 염원하는 빛의 광장이었다. 전국 사찰에서 모여든 불자와 연등 행렬에 참가했던 불자가 모두 이 광장에 모였다.

행사는 오후 7시쯤 동대문에서 출발해 종로를 통과한 연등 행렬이 광화문 광장으로 진입하면서 본격적으로 시작됐다.

사천왕상을 비롯해 각양각색으로 모양을 낸 대형 장식등 20여

개가 광장 양편으로 도열했다. 서서히 어둠이 내리면서 불자들이 손에 손에 든 연등은 부드럽게 광화문 광장을 밝히기 시작했다. 정부종합청사 건물 위에도 별 하나가 떠올랐다.

오후 7시 35분, 예불이 시작됐다.

"시심귀명례"로 시작하는 예불문에 이어 30만 명이 합송하는 《반야심경》과 "석가모니불" 정근 소리가 광화문 광장에 울려 퍼졌다. 광화문 광장 세종대왕 동상 앞에 설치된 법고(法鼓)가 "둥둥" 울리기 시작했다. 소리의 릴레이였다.

오후 8시 정각, 조계종 종정 진제 스님이 입장했다. 천진난만한 미소로 장난치는 어린 동자승 일곱 명이 진제 스님 앞을 인도했다. 단상의 외국 스님들도 스마트폰을 꺼내서 입장하는 진제 스님과 행사 모습을 촬영하느라 바쁜 모습이었다.

행사는 기원대회와 무차대회 두 가지 성격이 이어졌다. 그래서 단상에는 불교 각 종단 대표자 등과 한국 간화선을 상징하는 조계종의 각 선원장도 자리했다.

대형 화면을 통해 조계사의 범종이 평화의 염원을 담아 다섯 번 울리는 장면이 광장에 생중계되며 기원대회가 시작됐다.

조계종 총무원장 자승 스님은 '한반도 평화를 위한 2015 불교 통일 선언'을 발표했다. 연초부터 조계종이 머리를 맞대고 준비해온 선언이었다.

대원칙은 세 가지, 공존, 상생, 합심이었다.

자승 스님은 먼저 부처님이 제자들에게 던진 질문으로 첫머리를 열었다.

"너희는 서로 화목하고 다툼이 없으며 물과 우유처럼 서로 어울리고, 서로 사랑하고 서로 돌보며 사느냐?" 이어 "부처님의 이 질문 앞에서 한반도의 불자들은 자성과 참회의 마음을 감출 수 없다"고 했다.

그리고 '물과 우유처럼' 어울리기 위해서 "부처님의 가르침에서 길을 찾겠다", "공존과 상생은 차이를 인정하는 데서 출발한다", "합심은 마음의 본바탕인 '일심'을 살펴 진실한 의지를 합쳐 나가는 것"이라고 말했다. 그러면서 "불교도는 굳어져 버린 남북관계를 풀고 민족 동질성 회복과 통일의 대업을 이룩하는 데 앞장서겠다"고 다짐했다.

선정에 이어 비구·비구니와 남녀 불자 그리고 동자·동녀(童子·童女)들로부터 법을 청해 받은 종정 진제 스님이 법상에 올라 주장자(지팡이)를 들어 "옛 부처가 나기 전에 누가 우주의 주인공인고? 고요하고 고요해서 그 체성은 평안한지라. 온 세계가 한 집이요 정이 있고 정이 없는 모든 만물이 한 몸이로다" 하며 법어를 시작했다. 진제 스님은 "이 주인공은 천지 만물의 근본이요, 일체중생의 마음자리"라며 "이 근본 자리는 텅 비어 고요함이나 분명하고 분명한 자리이다. 온갖 망령된 생각을 내려놓는다면, 바로 그 자리가 본래의 마음자리며 본래의 참모습"이라고 말했다.

그는 또 마음공부의 여섯 가지 길로 보시·지계·인욕·정진·선정·지혜를 꼽았다. 약 20여 분간에 걸친 진제 스님의 법어를 마지막으로 이날 '한반도 통일과 세계 평화를 위한 기원대회- 세계 간화선 무차대회'는 막을 내렸다. 한국 불교가 광화문 광장에서 이런 대규모 행사를 한 것은 이날 행사 사회를 본 백담사 무금선원 유나 영진 스님의 말처럼 "1,600년 역사상 처음"이었다.

| 세계 간화선 무차대회 |

"이 세 마디에 모든 성인과 모든 도인께서 설하신 법문이 다 들어 있으니, 이것을 가려낼 줄 안다면 모든 성인과 모든 도인과 어깨를 나란히 할 것입니다. 그러면 여기에 답을 하실 분 있습니까?"

지난 16일 저녁 서울 광화문 광장은 잠시 선방(禪房)으로 변했다. '세계 간화선 무차대회'에서 법상에 앉은 조계종 종정 진제 스님이 선문답을 던진 것이다.

그가 말한 세 마디는 당나라의 대도인으로 통했던 방 거사 가족이 주고받은 말이다. 어느 날 방 거사가 "어렵고 어려움이여, 높은 나무 위에 일백 석이나 되는 기름통의 기름을 펴는 것과 같구나" 하자 아내가 "쉽고 쉬움이여, 일백 가지 풀 끝이 모두 불법의 진리이구나"라고 답했다. 그러자 딸은 "어렵지도 아니하고 쉽지도 아니함이여, 피곤하면 잠자고 목마르면 차를 마신다"고 했다. 진제 스님은 "만약 산승이 방 거사 일가족이 한마디씩 할 때 그 자리에 있었더라면, 좋은 차를 달여서 한 잔씩 드렸을 것"이라고 말했다. 그러고는 또 질문을 던졌다. "그러면 이 차를 한 잔씩 드린 것은 법문을 잘해서 드린 것입니까? 아니면 잘못해서 드린 것입니까?"

깨달음이란 언어가 끊어진 자리, 말로는 표현할 수 없는 경지다. 진제 스님은 이날 선방에서 선승들이 깨달음의 경지를 두고 주고받는 법거량의 일단을 보여줬다. 본래 무차대회란 '누구든 참석을 막지 않는 법회'라는 뜻. 이날 대회도 세계 20개국에서 고승들이 참가하고 국내에서도 스님들과 전국 사찰의 신도 등이 차별 없이 참석했다. 진제 스님이 질문을 던졌을 때 청중석에 있던 한 스님이 일어나 "악, 악" 소리 지르며 손뼉을 쳤다. 선승으로서 공부를 점검받으려는, 혹은 진제 스님의 법문에 다른 의견을 이야기하려는 것이었으리라. 보통의 법회였다면 두 선승 사이에 법거량이 벌어졌을지 모른다. 그러나 워낙 많은 인원이 모인 자리라 무대 위의 진제 스님에게까지는 들리지 않았다.

진제 스님은 이날 법문에서 "일상생활하는 가운데 '부모에게 나기 전에 어떤 것이 참나인가?' 이 화두를 들고 가나 오나 앉으나 서나 챙기고 의심해야 한다. 그래서 문득 일념 삼매에 들어 크게 죽었다가 홀연히 살아나게 되면 마침내 마음의 고향에 이르러 대지혜와 대안락, 대자유와 대평화를 영원토록 누리게 된다"며 간화선 수행을 당부했다.

Teaching by Master Jinje Echoes through Gwanghwamun Plaza

⟨Chosun Ilbo Report of 2015 Conference⟩

May 20, 2015
Reporter. **Kim Hansu**

"Clap, clap, clap"

On the evening of May 16th, 2015, three raps of a bamboo clapper echoed through Seoul's Gwanghwamun Plaza. In an instant, the plaza fell serenely quiet and still. Gwanghwamun Plaza, the very heart of South Korea's capital Seoul, is generally bustling with the usual cacophony of horns and human voices. At times, the plaza turns into a major site of conflict, with protesters and police squads in strife. However, on this day the plaza was peaceful and quiet. An estimated 300,000 people closed their eyes in meditation, concentrating on the sounds of their heart. Then came the moment of tranquility (samadhi), the highlight of the "Conference for World Peace and Harmony: The Great Equal Assembly of Ganhwa Seon." On this day,

Gwanghwamun became a plaza of great illumination filled with prayers for peace and wisdom. Buddhists from various temples around the nation and participants of the Lotus Lantern Parade were all assembled together.

The event kicked off with Lotus Lantern Parade which departed Dongdaemun Gate at about 7 p.m. The parade then passed through the streets of Jongno and arrived at Gwanghwamun Plaza.

Some twenty traditional giant lanterns, including the Four Heavenly Kings (protectors of the Dharma), lined up on each side of the main block, flaunting their beautiful vivid colors. As the sun began to set, thousands of small hand held lanterns brightened up Gwanghwamun Plaza while a brilliant shining star on top of the Integrated Government Building shone brightly from above.

The 7:30 p.m. Dharma service began with the prayer of "Jisimgwimyeong-ye (we pay heartfelt homage)," chanted solemnly in unison by the 300,000 member assembly. This was followed by recitation of the Heart Sutra and then chanting of "Sakyamunibul" (Sakyamuni Buddha), which resonated throughout the plaza. During chanting, the magnificent sound of a Dharma drum was heard in front of the statue of King Sejong the Great. Then, at 8:00, Seon Master Jinje, the Supreme Patriarch of the Jogye Order of Korean Buddhism, made his entrance on the stage. Escorted by *dongjaseung* (young novice monks) with brimming smiles. On the main stage, Buddhist leaders from around the world were enthusiastically taking photographs to preserve the memory of Master Jinje's grand entrance.

The event was divided into two parts, a conference wishing for world peace and harmony, and the Great Equal Assembly of Ganhwa Seon. Since the conference emphasized Buddhism, representatives of each Buddhist order and the directors of the Seon Meditation Centers that represent Ganhwa Seon were all seated at the main stage.

The conference officially commenced with five majestic soundings of the Dharma bell that echoed from Jogye-sa Temple, broadcast live on the grand screen at the main stage.

Most Venerable Jaseung, the president of the Jogye Order of

Korean Buddhism, proclaimed the "2015 Buddhist Declaration for Peace and Reunification on the Korean Peninsula." The fundamental principle of this declaration, which was prepared by the Jogye Order at the beginning of this year, was peaceful coexistence, mutually sustainable ways of life and unity of minds. Venerable Jaseung began with a question Buddha posed to his disciples, "Do you live together in harmony, mutual appreciation and agreeability, like milk and water mixed, regarding each other with eyes of love?" Venerable Jaseung then said, "Confronted with this question from the Buddha, Korean Buddhists cannot help but repent and self-reflect." He also stated, "In order to mix as milk and water, we must follow the path of BuddhaDharma." He continued, "Coexistence and mutually sustainable ways of life start with accepting each other's differences." He went on to say "The unity of minds can be achieved by combining the sincere intentions of both parties based on the understanding of 'one mind.' This is the original ground of mind."

In conclusion, Jaseung declared, "Here and now, Buddhists must take the lead in resolving the strained relationship between North and South Korea, in recovering national homogeneity, and in completing the great work of reunification."

A moment of tranquility (samadhi) followed Venerable Jaseung's declaration. Bhikkhu, Bhikkhuni, Upasaka, Upasika, boy and a girl came forth, requesting Master Jinje to turn the wheel of Dharma. Seon Master Jinje rose to his Dharma seat, raised the Dharma staff once and began his teaching. "Who was the master of the universe before Buddha was born? In deep tranquility the essence is at peace. The whole universe is of a single family. All sentient and insentient beings are of the same essence."

Master Jinje told the assembly, "This master is the foundation of all things in the universe, and the ground of the mind for all sentient beings. This original ground is inherently empty and filled with stillness, but has distinct clarity. If you immediately let go of all delusions, you reclaim your original mind, which is your true nature."

Master Jinje then presented the six paths we should take to realize our true self and attain great wisdom: generosity, ethics, patience, joyous effort, meditative concentration, and wisdom.

The 'conference came to an end with a twenty minute Dharma teaching by Master Jinje. As stated by Ven. Yeongjin, the Master of Ceremonies and the Rector from Baekdamsa Temple, this was the first time in 1,600 years of Korean Buddhist history for such a grand Buddhist conference had taken place in Gwanghwamun Plaza.

| Conference for World Peace and Reunification of Korea |

"Is there anyone here who can answer my questions?"

On the night of May 16th, Seoul's Gwanghwamun Plaza transformed into a Seon practice hall. Seated on the high Dharma seat, Master Jinje gave his discourse at the Great Equal Assembly of Ganhwa Seon. As part of his discourse, Master Jinje told the story of Layman Pang's family, Pang being a famous sage from Tang China.

As the story goes, "-one day, Layman Pang was resting at home with his family. He suddenly mumbled to his wife, "Difficult and difficult! It is like smearing the top of a tall tree with a hundred gallons of oil." His wife retorted, "Easy and easy! The truth of the BuddhaDharma is reflected on the tips of a hundred blades of grass." Lingzhou interrupted in a flash and said, "It's neither difficult nor easy. When I'm thirsty, I drink tea. When I'm tired, I sleep."

Master Jinje then said to the assembly, "These passages contain the Dharma talks taught by all enlightened sages of the past. If you can distinguish them, you will not only join the ranks of all the enlightened sages, but I will also appoint you the Spiritual Patriarch of Donghwa-sa Temple."

Master Jinje continued "If this mountain monk had been present when each member of Pang's family spoke their passage, I would have brewed good tea and offered a cup to each of them." He then inquired, "Is my tea offering adequate praise for their well-presented Dharma talks or an insult?"

This is because the Dharma of the utmost truth cannot be expressed with words. On this day, Seon-Master Jinje demonstrated one of the finest examples of how a Dharma dialogue is exchanged by practicing monks at Seon meditation schools.

The term "equal assembly" means it is a conference without discrimination where all are welcome. Therefore, international Buddhist leaders from some 20 countries, members of the Sangha throughout the nation and lay Buddhists from various temples all gathered without prejudice or bias. In response to Master Jinje's question, a monk from the audience suddenly stood up and shouted, "Auk, Auk!" while clapping his hands. Perhaps he wished to have his level of practice examined or to state his opinion on the teachings of the master. Although a Dharma debate between the two monks could have taken place, the monk's voice was not heard by the master.

Master Jinje emphasized the importance of practicing Ganhwa Seon with the following words:
"In your daily life, investigate the following *hwadu*,
What is your true self before you are born?

Build up doubt about this *hwadu* ceaselessly, whether coming or going, standing or sitting. You should engage and-return to this *hwadu* a thousand or tens of thousands of times a day. Suddenly, you will find yourself immersed in one-pointed concentration and dwell in a state akin to death. Then, you come back to life, arriving at your original mind. Thereafter you can enjoy great freedom, great wisdom, great comfort and great peace for all eternity."

세계종교인회의 참석자들과 함께
광복 70주년 한반도 통일과 세계 평화를 위한 세계 간화선 무차대법회, 2015

With participants of the Religious Conference for World Peace
The Conference for World Peace and Reunification of Korea
Great Equality Assembly of Ganhwa Seon (Seoul, 2015)

30만 사부대중 한반도 통일, 세계 평화 위해 합장

2015. 5. 20 〈중앙일보〉 **배은나** 객원기자

세계 간화선 무차대회
200여 불교지도자 현충원 참배
조계사 종각서 '평화의 종' 타종

　불기 2559(2015)년 5월 16일 토요일 오후 8시. 서울 광화문 광장에 30만 사부대중이 모였다. 광복 70주년을 맞아 대한불교조계종이 개최한 세계 간화선 무차대회 현장이다.
　조계종은 지난 15~18일에 걸쳐 '한반도 통일과 세계 평화 기원대회'와 '세계 간화선 무차대회'를 열렸다. 16일 오전 10시 200여 명의 불교 지도자가 현충원을 참배하는 것을 시작으로 오후 2시엔 그랜드힐튼 서울 호텔에서 세계 평화를 위한 종교인회의가 개최됐다.

　20여 명이 참여한 가운데 세계 평화를 위한 종교인의 역할에 대해 논의하고, 세계 평화 기원문을 채택했다. 이어 오후 8시에는 서

울 광화문 광장에서 세계 간화선 무차대회가 열리고, 17일에는 서울 조계사에서 한국전쟁 희생자를 위한 무차수륙대재가 열렸다.

이번 대회에는 대한불교조계종 종정 예하 진제법원 대종사와 캄보디아의 승왕 스님 등 세계적인 불교지도자 200여 명과 미국, 프랑스, 호주 등에서 활동하는 종교지도자들이 동참했다. 조계종 측은 이번 대회의 핵심은 수행자를 비롯해 일반 대중 누구나 차별 없이 참여할 수 있다는 점이라고 밝혔다.

세계 간화선 무차대회는 백담사 유나 영진 스님의 사회로 막이 올랐다. 광화문 세종대왕상 뒤편 소무대에서 스님 두 명이 법고(불교 의식에 사용되는 북)를 시연했다.

중앙무대에는 종정 예하가 꽃을 한 송이씩 든 동자승 일곱 명과 등장했다. 종정 예하는 동자승 두 명을 각각 한 손에 잡고 입장했다. 동자승 일곱 명이 앞서가는 것은 아기 부처가 태어난 후 일곱 걸음을 걸었다는 것을 상징한 것이다. 종정 예하와 동자승 두 명의 입장은 한반도 통일과 세계 평화를 통해 미래 세대에 희망을 선사하자는 것을 상징화했다. 동자승이 퇴장하자 1만여 스님과 30만 불자들은 광화문에 울려 퍼지는 평화의 타종을 함께 들었다. 평화의 타종은 세계 평화를 기원하는 5타를 울렸다. 조계사 종각에서 타종하고, 이를 광화문 광장에서 생중계로 지켜봤다.

종이 울리고 조계종 총무원장 자승 스님이 한반도 평화를 위한

2015년 불교 통일 선언문을 낭독했다. 자승 스님은 법석을 연 종정 예하를 향해 깊은 공경을 올리고, 참석한 대중에게 감사 인사를 했다. 자승 스님은 "네팔에서 발생한 지진으로 희생되신 모든 영령의 극락왕생을 기원하며 그들의 가족과 네팔 모든 국민이 위기극복을 위해 지혜와 용기를 잃지 않기를 기도하자"고 말했다. 또한 "대한민국 국민들 또한 세월호 사건을 겪으며 견딜 수 없는 고통을 함께 나눴다"면서 세월호의 교훈을 되새겨 신뢰하는 공동체가 되기를 기원했다. 자승 스님은 "한반도 통일과 세계 평화를 이루는 과정은 '참나'를 찾는 수행의 과정과 같다. 오늘 참석한 대중 모두 온전한 삶의 주인공이 되고 세상의 주인이 되어 평화의 길을 열어나가자"고 덧붙였다.

한반도 통일선언이 끝나고 영상을 통해 박근혜 대통령의 축하 메시지가 전달됐다.

종정 예하의 법어를 앞두고 사부대중은 죽비 소리와 함께 선정(禪定)에 들었다. 고요하고 장엄한 침묵이 이어졌다. 종정 예하 진제법원 대종사는 사람이 곧 부처임을 깨달아 서로 존중하고 상생하는 삶을 사는 일이 이 자리에 있는 우리가 이뤄야 할 서원"이라고 법어를 내렸다.

마지막 순서는 세계 종교지도자들의 평화 기원 선언이었다. 외국인 스님들과 어린이 30여 명이 무대에서 평화와 희망을 담은 노래를 합창했다. 상처투성이 광화문 광장에 평온함이 깃드는 밤이었다.

Three Hundred Thousand Korean Buddhists Pray for World Peace and Reunification of Korea

⟨Joongang Ilbo Report of 2015 Conference⟩

May 20, 2015
Guest Reporter. **Bae Eunna**

The Buddhist Assembly of South Korea came together in Seoul's Gwanghwamun Plaza on the evening of Saturday May 16th to mark the 70th anniversary of Korea's independence from Japanese colonial rule and hold the Great Equal Assembly of Ganhwa Seon, which was organized by the Jogye Order of Korean Buddhism.

The Jogye Order's Conference for World Peace and Reunification of Korea: Great Equal Assembly of Ganhwa Seon was held from May 15th to May 18th. Over 200 international Buddhist leaders from 20 foreign countries began the program by paying tribute at Seoul National Cemetery. Twenty interreligious leaders from across the globe then attended the Meeting of Religious

Members for World Peace at the Seoul Grand Hilton Hotel. The leaders discussed the role of religious must play in realizng world peace and created a declaration outlining a plant to attain world peace. At 8:00p.m. on the same day, the Great Equal Assembly of Ganhwa Seon commenced followed by the Great Equal Water and Land Ceremony in Jogye-sa Temple the next morning.

Among the attendees were Jinje Beopwon, the Supreme Patriarch of the Jogye Order, Tep Vong, the Supreme Patriarch of Cambodia, over 200 international Buddhist leaders and other religious leaders from various nations including the United States, France and Australia.

The Jogye Order stated during the public announcement, "The essence of this conference is for the public, including Buddhists, to participate without discrimination or unfairness."

The assembly of Ganhwa Seon began with Ven. Yeongjin from Baekdam-sa Temple speaking as the master of ceremonies. A traditional drumming ceremony by two Bhikkhus then followed on a stage behind the statue of King Sejong the Great.

Master Jinje then entered the central stage led by seven

dongjaseung, who symbolized the first seven steps Buddha took on earth. During his entrance, Master Jinje held the hands of two of the *dongjaseung* as an offering of hope to future generations for world peace and reunification of the Korean Peninsula. After the *dongjaseung* left the stage, ten thousand members of the assembly and over 300,000 Buddhists heard the sounding of the Bell of Peace, which was struck five times with aspiration for world peace. The majestic Dharma bell echoed from the Jogye-sa bell pavilion, while the public viewed it live at Gwanghwamun Plaza.

After the bell ceremony, the president of the Jogye Order, Most Venerable Jaseung, recited the 2015 Buddhist Declaration for Peace and Reunification on the Korean Peninsula. The president offered his deepest gratitude to Master Jinje for gathering Dharma assembly and extended his appreciation to the virtuous monastics who came from abroad and to all those present. Ven. Jaseung stated in the declaration, "I pray for the spirits of those who lost their lives in the disastrous earthquakes of Nepal to be reborn in the Pure Land, and for all the citizens of Nepal, including the families of the victims to overcome this crisis with wisdom and courage." He then added, "Korean citizens also share unbearable suffering in the aftermath of the Sewol Ferry disaster. Taking a lesson from this painful accident, I hope Korea may progress onward to a safer and more trustworthy society."

Ven. Jaseung further stated, "The process of realizing Korea's reunification and world peace is similar to the Buddhist path of seeking the true self and I pray that all of you here today may become the rightful master of your lives and of the world, and open the path of peace."

After the declaration, a congratulatory video message from South Korean president Park Geunhye was shown.

The assembly then sat in solemn silence before Master Jinje began his teaching. Seon Master Jinje taught, "…to realize that a person is a Buddha and to respect and live a mutually sustainable life are the vows we must make today."

Finally, the "2015 Buddhist Declaration for Peace" was recited by the world religious leaders. Some thirty children along with the international sangha then gathered on the stage to sing songs of peace and hope. On that night, the pain and suffering witnessed by Gwanghwamun Plaza in the past was forgotten.

광화문 대법회장 광경

The Conference for World Peace and Reunification of Korea

CNN의 행사현장 TV 보도

CNN TV Report
Great Equality Assembly of Ganhwa Seon (Seoul, 2015)

대한불교 조계종 종정 진제 스님
한반도 통일을 꿈꾸다

2015. 5. 18
〈CNN〉 캐시 노벡 기자

수십만 불자들 모여 평화통일 기원

 대한민국의 심장인 서울 광화문 광장에 서서히 어둠이 깔리자 시끄러운 도시의 소음은 수십만 사람들의 평화로운 합송과 정근 소리로 변해서 광장에 울려 퍼졌다.
 현지 16일 토요일 저녁, 30만 명의 불자가 대한민국의 수도인 서울 광화문 광장에 모여 세계 평화와 한반도 통일을 기원했다.
 광복 70주년을 맞아 개최된 세계 간화선 무차대회에 세계 각국의 불교 지도자들이 동참했다.
 한국 불교를 대표하는 대한불교조계종의 종정인 진제 대선사와 어렵게 이루어진 인터뷰 회견에서 종정 진제 대선사는 이번 행사가 광복 70주년을 기념하고 평화 통일을 기원하는 법회라고 말했다.

 종정 스님은 "한반도 분단은 많은 사람에게 슬픔을 안겨주고 있다. 이 문제를 해결하기 위해서 이번 세계 간화선 무차대법회는 한반도 통일에 중점을 두고 있다. 간화선을 통해 세계 인류에 평화를 가져다주기 위해서이다"라고 전했다.

한국 그 자체는 특별히 종교국가라 할 수 없지만 2014년 한국갤럽조사연구소에 의하면 한국인의 약 20%가 불자이며 진제 대선사는 한국의 가장 중요한 정신적 지도자이다.

근교 도시인 성남시에서 대회에 참석한 황 씨는 "부처님의 대자비가 모든 곳에 펼쳐져 우리 모두가 하나되어 평화통일이 실현되길 기원합니다"라고 전했다.

종정 진제 스님은 "500년의 불교 역사가 북한사람 모두의 마음에 남아있다"고 전하며 "우리는 항상 상부상조의 관계를 맺고 있으며 미래에는 많은 이들의 마음을 열 기회가 있을 것이다. 그러므로 우리는 북한을 배척하기보다는 서로를 도와야 한다"고 말했다.

또 "최근 중국에서 남북한 지도자들이 만났고 불자들은 북한에 있는 불교사찰을 복원하기 위해 많은 노력을 기하고 있다. 남한 불자들이 북쪽 구호활동에도 더욱 힘쓸 것"이라고 말했다.

그러나 종정 진제 스님은 불교가 어떻게 더욱 적극적인 역할을 해나갈 계획인지에 대해서는 언급하지 않았다. 아마도 프란치스코 교황 방문 이후 바티칸이 쿠바와 미국의 상호 관계를 회복시킨 것이나, 독일 교회가 국가의 통일에 중추적인 역할을 한 것과 같은 방식을 택할 수도 있을 것이다. 하지만 진제 대선사는 더욱 영적인 방식을 선호했다.

"우리 모두가 수행을 일상화할 때 마음속에 있는 모든 갈등이 해소될 수 있다. 이러한 생각을 남북한 사람들의 마음에 심어주면 모든 시기와 질투, 분쟁이 사라질 것이라고 확신한다. 남북한의 통일도 더욱 빨리 실현될 것이다." 종정 진제 스님은 평화는 내면에서부터 이루어지는 것이라고 말했다.

Reunification is a Dream for South Korea's Buddhist Patriarch

⟨CNN Report of 2015 Conference⟩

May 18, 2015,
CNN, Reporter. **Kathy Novak**

Seoul (CNN) As the sun set over South Korea's capital, the usual cacophony of sounds associated with a bustling major city was replaced by human voices – hundreds of thousands of them, chanting peacefully.

An estimated 300,000 Buddhists descended on central Seoul on Saturday evening local time, packing the streets around the Gyeongbokgung – the main royal palace – to pray for peace and reunification with the North.

The event was staged to mark the 70th anniversary of Korean independence, and it brought together Buddhist leaders from around the world.

In a rare interview with CNN, the spiritual leader of the Jogye Order of Korean Buddhism – the country's largest sect – the

Supreme Patriarch Jinje, said it was also the anniversary of Korea's separation.

"The separation has been causing pain for the people," he said.

"To solve this problem, we are focusing on peace for the Koreas during this Buddhism meditation assembly. The purpose of this meditation is to bring peace to all the people – people of the whole world."

South Koreans on the whole are not particularly religious. But for the approximately 20 percent of South Koreans who practice Buddhism – according to a 2014 study by Gallup Korea – Master Jinje is a key spiritual figure.

Hwang Yeon-gyeong traveled from Seongnam on the outskirts of Seoul to join in the event. "With the mercy of Buddha, we should come together as the same people and I hope we can realize peaceful reunification." she said.

US Secretary of State John Kerry is in Seoul to discuss security on the peninsula. With North and South Korea technically still at war, recent reports out of Pyongyang have done little to ease tensions and anxiety south of the demilitarised zone that separates the two neighbors. "In North Korea, there are 500 years of Buddhism rooted in every person's heart," he said.

"We are carrying the spirit of mutual help and I believe there will be opportunities for people to open up their hearts in the future. That is why we should not neglect, but rather help each other." He said leaders from the North and South met recently in China and that Buddhists had been working to restore temples in the North. Korean Buddhists also promised more humanitarian aid programmes.

But the Supreme Patriarch would not expand on whether Buddhists planned to play a more active role – perhaps take a leaf out of Pope Francis' book, after the Vatican's contribution to bettering relations between Cuba and the United states; or look to the pivotal role German church leaders played during that country's reunification. But his approach is more spiritual.

"When we practice our daily asceticism," he said. "we make all conflicts in our heart disappear. "By instilling these ideas in all people and the people of the two Koreas, I'm confident that all envy and conflict will disappear and that the reunification of the two Koreas will be quickly realised." For the Buddhist leader, peace begins from within.

광화문 대법회장 광경
광복 70주년 한반도 통일과 세계 평화를 위한 세계 간화선 무차대법회, 2015

The Conference for World Peace and Reunification of Korea
The Great Equality Assembly of Ganhwa Seon at Gwanghwamun Plaza (Seoul, 2015)

팔공총림 동화사 방장 승좌(昇座) 대법회, 2013

Dharma assembly for the Spiritual Patriarch (Bangjang) Installation Ceremony at
Palgong Comprehensive Monastic Training Complex (Daegu, 2013)

덕산탁발화 암두밀계기의
(德山托鉢話 岩頭密啓其意)

2015.6.1. 을미년 하안거 결제 법어, 동화사

[상당하시어 주장자를 들어 대중에게 보이시고]

태평세월에 업을 다스리는 데는 상이 없음이요,
들늙은이들의 가풍은 지극히 순함이라.
다못 촌에서 노래하고 모여서 마시는지라.
이에 순임금의 덕과 요임금의 어짊을 어찌 아리오.

태평치업무상(太平治業無像)이요
야노가풍지순(野老家風至淳)이라.
지관촌가사음(只管村歌社飲)하니
나지순덕요인(那知舜德堯仁)이리요.

 금일은 을미년 하안거(夏安居) 결제일이라. 모든 결제대중은 부처님께서 사바(娑婆)에 출세하신 뜻을 좇아 일구월심(日久月深) 참나를 밝히는 일에 몰두해야 함이로다. 우리가 세속의 온갖 부귀영화를 마다하고 일가 친족 등 정(情)으로 맺은 모든 인연을 다 끊고 출가하여 먹물 옷을 입고 있는 것은 오로지 나고 죽는 고통을 영구히 여의고자 하는 데 있지 다른 데 있는 것이 아니로다. 그런데 이 일은 남이 대신해줄 수 있는 것도 아니요, 어디 다른 나라에 가서 가져올 수 있는 것도 아니니, 오직 스스로 닦아서 스스로 증득(證得)해야 함이로다.

불가에는 여러 수행법이 있지만 다른 여타의 수행법으로는 대오견성(大悟見性)이 불가능하고 오직 간화선 수행만이 이 일을 밝혀줄 수 있으니, 다겁생에 만나기 힘든 이 견성법(見性法)을 만난 김에 이번 생은 태어나지 않은 셈 치고 수행에 몰두해야 함이로다.

그러면 어떻게 닦아야 참나를 밝혀 생사(生死)를 요달(了達)할 수 있음인고?

화두가 있는 이는 각자 화두를 챙기되, 화두가 없는 이는 "부모에게 나기 전에 어떤 것이 참나인가?"

하는 이 화두를 들고 오매불망(寤寐不忘) 간절히 의심하고 의심해야 함이로다. 화두를 챙기고 의심을 쭈욱 밀어주기를 하루에도 천 번 만 번 반복해서, 마음에서 우러나오는 간절한 화두의심 한 생각이 끊어짐이 없도록 혼신을 다해 참구해야 함이로다.

앞서 화두를 참구할 때는 자세가 반듯해야 하는 것이니, 가슴을 활짝 펴고, 허리를 반듯이 곧게 세우고, 눈은 보통으로 뜨되 2미터 앞 아래에다 시야를 고정해 두고 화두를 챙겨야 함이로다. 화두 의심에 용을 써서 몸에 힘이 들어가면 상기(上氣)가 되어 머리가 무거워져서 참선할 수 없게 되니, 오직 생각으로만 화두를 챙기고 간절한 의심을 밀어주어야 함이로다.

이렇게 바른 자세로 뼛골에 사무치는 의심을 짓고 화두를 챙겨 가면, 사위의(四威儀) 가운데 눈앞에 화두가 떠나지 않아 졸리는 것도 없고 망상이 일어날래야 일어날 수가 없으니, 자신도 모르는 사이에 공부가 무르익어지는 것이로다.

그렇게 혼신의 정력을 쏟아 무한히 노력하다 보면 문득 참의심 이 발동하여 화두의심 한 생각만이 또렷이 드러나게 되는데, 가나 오나 앉으나 서나 밥을 지으나 청소를 하나 일을 하나 잠을 자나, 일체처일체시(一切處一切時)에 화두 한 생각만 흐르는 냇물처럼 끊어짐 없이 흘러가게 됨이니, 사물을 봐도 본 줄을 모르고 소리를 들어도 들은 줄을 모르게 되어 다겁다생(多劫多生)에 지어온 모든 습기(習氣)가 다 녹아 없어져 버리게 됨이로다.

이러한 상태로 한 달이고 일 년이고 시간이 흐르고 흐르다가 홀 연히 사물을 보는 찰나에, 소리를 듣는 찰나에 화두가 박살이 남 과 동시에 자기의 참모습이 환히 드러나게 되는 것이로다. 그러면 한 걸음도 옮기지 않고 여래(如來)의 땅에 이르게 되고 천칠백공안 (千七百公案)을 한 꼬챙이에 다 꿰어버리게 되는 것이니, 누가 어 떠한 법문을 물어 와도 척척 바른 답을 내놓게 되는 것이로다.

이것이 바로 호왈견성(號曰見性)이요, 확철대오(廓徹大悟)인지라, 반드시 선지식을 친견하여 바르게 점검받아서 인가(印可)를 받아야 함이로다.

왜 그러한가?

광대무변한 진리의 세계는 혼자서는 도저히 다 알았다고 할 수 없기에 반드시 먼저 깨달은 눈 밝은 선지식을 의지해서 점검과 인가를 받아야 하는 것이로다. 그래서 부처님께서도 "무사자오(無師自悟)는 천마외도(天魔外道)다" 즉, 정법을 이은 선지식으로부터 점검받은 바 없이 깨달았다 하는 자는 천마외도일 뿐이라고 못을 박아놓으신 것이로다.

이렇듯 대오견성하기 위해서는 선지식의 지도 아래 철두철미한 신심으로 간절하게 의심하며 화두를 챙겨가야 함이로다.

그러니 모든 대중은 이 같은 자세로써 어떻게든 이번 안거(安居) 동안에 득력(得力)하여 불은(佛恩)과 시은(施恩)을 다 갚고 생사를 요달(了達)할 수 있도록 혼신의 정력을 쏟을지어다.

석일(昔日)에 덕산(德山) 선사께서 회상(會上)을 열어 대중을 지도하고 계실 때, 참으로 훌륭한 두 분의 눈 밝은 제자를 두었다. 한 분은 암두(岩頭) 선사인데 참선하여 깨달은 바도 없이 그대로 생이지지(生而知之)요, 또 한 분은 훗날 천오백 대중을 거느리신 설봉(雪峰) 선사였다.

하루는 덕산 선사께서 공양 시간이 되지 않았는데 발우(鉢盂)를

들고 공양간으로 걸어가셨다. 공양주인 설봉 스님이 이 모습을 보고 여쭙기를,

"방장 스님, 종도 치지 않고 북도 울리지 않았는데 발우를 가지고 어디로 가십니까?"

하니, 덕산 선사께서는 아무 말도 없이 그냥 고개를 숙이고 조실방으로 돌아가 버리셨다.

그 광경을 설봉 스님이 사형(師兄)되는 암두 스님에게 말하니, 암두 스님이 듣고는 대뜸 말했다.

"덕산 노인이 말후구(末後句) 진리를 알지 못하는구나!"

자신의 스승이건만 단번에 이렇게 평가하니 법을 논함에 있어서는 스승과 제자를 따지지 않는 법이로다. 덕산 선사께서 아무 말 없이 고개를 숙이고 돌아간 뜻이 무엇이며, 암두 스님은 어째서 덕산 선사가 말후구 진리를 알지 못했다 했는지 알아야 함이로다.

암두 스님의 그 말이 총림에 분분하여 덕산 선사의 귀에 들어가니 암두 스님을 불러서 물으시기를,

"너는 왜 내가 말후구를 알지 못했다고 하는고?"

하시니, 암두 스님이 덕산 선사의 귀에다 대고 아무도 듣지 못하게 은밀히 속삭였다.

그런 후로 뒷날 덕산 선사께서 상당하시어 법문하시는데 종전과 판이하게 다르고 당당하게 법문하셨다.

법문을 다 마치시고 법상에서 내려오니, 암두 스님이 덕산 선사의 손을 잡고,

"정말 반갑고 즐겁습니다. 스님의 법은 천하 도인이라도 당할 자가 없습니다. 그러나 3년밖에 세상에 머물지 못합니다."

하니, 덕산 선사는 과연 3년 후에 열반(涅槃)에 드셨다.

암두 스님이 덕산 선사의 귀에 대고 은밀히 속삭인 대문을 알겠는가?

대체 무엇이라고 속삭였기에 덕산 선사께서 종전과는 판이하고 당당한 법문을 하신 것인가?

'덕산탁발화(德山托鉢話)' 이 공안은 백천공안(百千公案) 가운데 가장 알기가 어려운 법문인지라, 천하 선지식도 바로 보기가 어려워 이 법문에 대해서 평을 한 이가 거의 없음이로다. 그래서 이 공안을 바로 보는 눈이 열려야 대오견성을 했다고 인정함이로다.

그러면 금일 모든 결제대중은 알겠는가?

[한참을 계시다 대중이 말이 없음에 이르시기를]

산승이 양팔을 걷어붙이고 이 법문을 점검해서 천하에 공개하리니, 어째서 이와 같이 점검하였는지 대중은 잘 살필지어다.

한 망아지가 천하 사람을 밟아 죽이니,
그 위대한 임제 선사도 백염적이 되지 못함이로다.

마구답살천하인(馬駒踏殺天下人)하니
임제미시백염적(臨濟未是白拈賊)이로다.

[주장자로 법상을 한 번 치고 하좌하시다.]

손에 연등을 들고 행진하는 참가자들
광복 70주년 한반도 통일과 세계 평화를 위한 세계 간화선 무차대법회, 2015

Conference participants walking along Jongno Street, each carrying a lotus lantern
The Conference for World Peace and Reunification of Korea
Great Equality Assembly of Ganhwa Seon (Seoul, 2015)

Deshan Carrying His Bowls

Beginning of the 2015 summer retreat at Donghwa-sa Temple

[The Master ascends the Dharma Seat and shows the Dharma Staff to the assembly.]

> **To purify karma at the time of great peace has no sign**
> **The family way of the old peasants is most pristine**
> **Only concerned with village songs and festival drinking,**
> **How would they know of the virtues of Shun or the benevolence of Yao?**

Today is the beginning of the summer retreat for 2015, the year of the sheep. Every one of you who has gathered here to participate in the retreat must join the Buddha's quest to illuminate your true self day and night. Our decision to wear the grey robe (robe of monastics), which means to let go of any desire for wealth and honor in this mundane world and to sever all ties with friends and family, leaving us only one goal in life: to overcome the suffering of birth and death. But, no one else can do this for you, nor can you find it in a foreign land. You alone must cultivate your mind and attain it for yourself.

Various practices exist in Buddhism, but there is no better path than Ganhwa Seon to attain great awakening, and it is the sole practice that can illuminate the path of truth. So rare and difficult is it for one to encounter this path of Dharma and see the true nature of mind that the opportunity may not come again for another million lifetimes. Thus, pretend as if you had never been born and devote yourself wholly to your practice.

Then, how can we awaken the true self and resolve this matter of life and death in this lifetime? If you have already received a *hwadu*, investigate it. If you do not have a *hwadu* yet, take the *hwadu*, "What is your true self before you are born of your parents?"

Hold this *hwadu* at all times, fervently investigating and doubting it without ever forgetting it. With tens and thousands of repeated questions on the *hwadu* with single-minded concentration, your earnest doubt on the *hwadu* must flow unceasingly.

How can you do this correctly? It is important to maintain proper posture when investigating your *hwadu*. Thus, sit with your back straight, expand your chest, look at the floor six feet in front of you and focus on your *hwadu*. If bodily tension increases with your effort, your energy will flow in reverse resulting in "fire" energy rising to your head. This induces a feeling of heaviness, making it impossible to continue Seon practice. Thus, devote yourself wholly to the *hwadu* in your mind only, and build on your doubt.

With effort desperate enough to penetrate to the bone, you must be able to focus on your *hwadu* whether you are walking, standing, sitting or lying down. With an earnest mind welling up from the depths of your heart, the *hwadu* will linger in front of your eyes at all times, and you must not succumb to drowsiness or distracting thoughts. Your practice will soon ripen without your even being aware of it. In this way, when true doubt is set in motion, single-minded focus on the *hwadu* flows clearly and without disruption. Whether you are coming or going, sitting or standing, cooking or cleaning, at work or asleep, only the singular thought of the *hwadu* will flow at all times, like the running waters of a stream. At this time, even if objects are visible, you don't have any sense of seeing them; even if sounds are audible, you don't have any sense of hearing them. Immersed in this state, your karma of thousands and millions of past lives will all melt away. In this state, a month or a year may pass. Then suddenly, the opportune time comes, and you will see an object or hear a sound, and your *hwadu* will shatter; you will penetrate it and your true self will be illuminated. Then, you will reach the Pure Land of the Buddha without having taken a single step and pierce all 1,700 *gongans* with a single skewer, being able to answer any question that comes your way.

That is what we refer to as seeing one's true nature and attaining perfect enlightenment where all darkness and defilements dissipate with the rising of the sun. But, afterward, you must meet an authentic, clear-eyed teacher to have him assess your level of attainment and receive his seal of approval. Why is this so?

The mind's true home is so vast and boundless, profound and recondite, that it is almost impossible for one to appraise on one's own whether one has attained it or not. You must depend on your Seon master and be examined and approved by him. That is why the Buddha stressed in no uncertain terms: "To claim that one has attained the Path of Truth without the guidance of an enlightened master is a sure way of becoming a mara or heretic." One must not speak of one's own enlightenment without a teacher's seal of approval. As can be seen, to attain great awakening, one must study diligently under the tutelage of a Seon master and question one's *hwadu* earnestly.

Always maintain this attitude, vow to attain great awakening during this retreat and repay your debt of gratitude for the benevolence of the Buddha and your patrons. With all the power you can muster, you must be ready to conquer the cycle of life and death.

Once when Seon Master Deshan (德山) was leading a Dharma assembly, he had under him two outstanding disciples who possessed the great bright wisdom eye. One was Yantou (岩頭), born with the eye of wisdom and already a learned being at birth, and the other was Xuefeng (雪峰), who would eventually come to teach 1,500 monks.

One day, when it was not yet meal time, Seon Master Deshan came to the dining hall carrying his alms bowl. Xuefeng, who was in charge of cooking the meals, saw him and asked, "Where are you going with your alms bowl when the bell has not yet been rung nor the drum struck?" Hearing this, Master Deshan hung his head and returned to his room in silence. When Xuefeng relayed what happened to Deshan's senior disciple, Yantou, Yantou cockily replied, "Deshan, the pathetic old teacher does not know the Final Phrase of the Supreme Truth."

Appraising his own master without hesitation, a proper Dharma dialogue should not distinguish between who is the teacher and who is the disciple. Why did Master Deshan hang his head and return to his room when asked, "Where are you going with your alms bowls when the bell has not yet been rung nor the drum struck?" One must also understand why Yantou said Deshan does not know the Final Phrase of the Supreme Truth.

Yantou's remark caused quite a stir in the assembly. The Master summoned and admonished Yantou. "Why did you say that I did not know the Final Phrase of the Supreme Truth?" Yantou whispered secretly into Master Deshan's ear what his comment meant. The next day, Seon Master Deshan gave an extraordinary Dharma talk, completely unlike any of his past teachings. When the Master finished and descended from the Dharma seat, Yantou, still rejoicing at the talk, held the Master's hands and said: "How wonderful! Now that the Master has attained the Final Phrase of the Supreme Truth, your lofty Dharma will be unsurpassed for ages to come. Unfortunately, your time in this life will come to an end in a mere three years." And in fact, Master Deshan entered parinirvana after the predicted three years had passed.

Everyone in the assembly! If any of you truly understand the meaning of why Master Yantou whispered into Master Deshan's ear, let's hear it! What did Master Yantou whisper for Master Deshan to give such an extraordinary teaching afterward? This story of "Deshan Holds Up His Bowl" has been the subject of heated debate for a long time. It was a teaching of such deep insight and profound truth that it was often incomprehensible, even to many masters of sterling reputation. Only masters who had attained the truly bright wisdom eye were able to engage in Seon dialogue based on this *gongan*.

Members of the assembly gathered here today, do you understand?

[The Master awaits and addresses the silent assembly,]

This mountain monk will now examine and explain the meaning of this teaching. Assembly, now try to discern the answer.

A horse in its prime tramples everyone on earth to death.

Linji cannot yet steal without leaving behind a clue.

[The Master hits the Dharma staff once and descends the Dharma Seat.]

봉암사 조실 추대식 상당법문

The Supreme Patriarch Installation Ceremony held at Bongam-sa Temple

조주 선사와 황벽 선사, 임제 선사의 거량(擧揚)

2015.8.28. 을미년 하안거 해제 법어, 동화사

동화사에서 해제 법어 중인 종정 예하
Master Jinje gives a Dharma Teaching at Donghwa-sa Temple

[상당하시어 주장자를 들어 대중에게 보이시고.]

이 주장자 진리를 알 것 같으면
줄탁의 기틀은 화살과 칼날을 잡음이니,
눈 깜짝할 사이에 손과 주인을 가림이로다.
이 주장자 진리를 알지 못한다 하더라도
주장자 머리 위에 해와 같은 밝은 눈이 있어서
한인(漢人)을 만나면 한인을 나투고,
호인(胡人)을 만나면 호인을 나툼이로다.

식득주장자(識得拄杖子)하면
줄탁지기전추봉(啐啄之機箭抽鋒)이니
별연빈주찰나분(瞥然賓主刹那分)이라.
불식주장자(不識拄杖子)라도
장두유안명여일(杖頭有眼明如日)하여
한래한현호래호현(漢來漢現胡來胡現)이라.

   금일은 어언 여름 석 달 안거(安居)를 마치는 하안거 해제일(夏安居 解制日)이라.
   결제(結制)에 임했던 기상과 기개로 삼복더위를 잊고 각고의 정진에 몰두해서 본분사(本分事)를 해결했다면 금일이 진정한 해제가 될 것이나, 그렇지 못하다면 해제일이 동시에 결제일이 되어야 할 것이다. 자신을 돌아보고 돌아보아야 함이로다.

　진정한 해제란 화두를 타파하여 자기의 본성을 알게 될 때 천하를 종횡(縱橫)하는 대자유인(大自由人)이 되는 것이다. 그렇지 않나면 다시금 마음을 담금질하여 대오견성(大悟見性)의 각오(覺悟)를 되새겨야 할 것이다.
　해제일이 되었다고 바랑을 지고 이산 저산을 유랑 다니듯이 정신없이 다녀서는 아니 될 것이며, 화두를 걸망에 넣어두고 허깨비처럼 행각(行脚)을 떠나서도 아니 될 것이다.
　그렇게 허송세월만 보내서는 대도(大道)를 이루기가 불가능하니 화두를 타파하여 선지식께 인가받는 날이 해제라 다짐하고 바위처럼 흔들림이 없이 혼신의 힘으로 정진(精進)에 정진을 거듭해야 함이로다.

　화두를 챙김에 있어 일거수일투족이 마음에서 우러나와서, 걸음걸음마다 호흡 호흡마다 화두를 여의지 않고 간절한 마음으로 화두를 챙기고 의심하기를 흐르는 물과 같이 끊어짐이 없도록 씨름해야 할 것이로다.

　이렇게 일념(一念)이 되도록 노력하다 보면 문득 참의심이 돈발(頓發)하여 보는 것도 잊어버리고, 듣는 것도 잊어버리고, 밤인지 낮인지도 모르고 며칠이고 몇 달이고 흐르고 흐르다가 홀연히 사물을 보는 찰나에, 소리를 듣는 찰나에, 화두가 해결되어 불조(佛祖)의 백천공안(百千公案)을 한 꼬챙이에 꿰어 버리게 됨이니. 그러면 누가 어떤 물음을 던지더라도 석화전광(石火電光)으로 척척 바른 답을 내놓게 되고, 제불제조(諸佛諸祖)와 조금도 다를 바 없는 살림살이를 수용하게 될 것이다.

이렇게 되면 억만년(億萬年)이 다하도록 깨달은 삼매(三昧)의 낙(樂)을 누리고 염라대왕이 잡으러 온다 해도 보이지 않으니 잡아갈 수가 없음이로다.

석일(昔日)에 조주(趙州) 선사께서 행각차(行脚次) 황벽(黃檗) 선사 회상에 들르시니, 황벽 선사께서 조주 선사 오시는 것을 보시고는 방장실(方丈室)로 들어가 문을 닫아 버리셨다. 이에 조주 선사께서 법당(法堂)에 들어가서

"구화구화(救火救火, 불이야! 불이야!)!"

하시니, 황벽 선사께서 문을 열고 나와서 조주 선사를 붙잡고 말씀하셨다.

"도도하라!(道道하라, 일러라! 일러라!)"

이에 조주 선사께서

"적과후장궁(賊過後張弓, 도적이 지나간 후에 활을 쏨)이라."

하셨다.

일일(一日)에 조주 선사께서 임제사(臨濟寺)를 방문하여 발을 씻

고 있는 차에, 임제 선사께서 다가와 물으시기를,

"어떤 것이 조사가 서쪽에서 오신 뜻입니까?"

하시니, 조주 선사께서

"마침 노승이 발을 씻는 중이니라."

하고 대답하셨다. 이에 임제 선사께서 가만히 다가가서 귀를 기울이고 들으시거늘, 조주 선사께서

"알면 바로 알 것이지, 되씹어 무엇하려는고?"

하심에 임제 선사께서 팔을 흔들며 가버리시니, 조주 선사께서 말씀하셨다.

"30년간 행각(行脚)하다가 오늘에야 처음으로 주각(注脚)을 잘못 내렸다."

시회대중(時會大衆)은 조주 선사를 알겠는가?

[한참을 계시다 대중이 말이 없으니, 스스로 점검하여 이르시기를]

조주 선사는 모름지기 위를 뚫고 아래를 뚫어보는 눈을 갖추어서
처처에 선지식을 상봉하니
기틀에 다다른 일구가 천고에 빛남이로다.

수구투정투저지안(須具透頂透底之眼)하야
처처상봉선지식(處處相逢善知識)하니

당기일구천고휘(當機一句千古輝)로다.

대중은 황벽 선사를 알겠는가?

용과 범이 서로 부딪힘에 전신을 회피하기가 어려운지라.
비록 이와 같으나
능란한 솜씨에 능란한 솜씨를 바치니,
천상세계와 인간세계에 몇몇이나 될꼬?

용호상박 전신회피난(龍虎相撲 全身廻避難)이라.
수연여시(雖然如是)나
호수중 정호수(好手中 呈好手)하니
천상인간능기기(天上人間能幾幾)냐?

대중은 임제 선사를 알겠느냐?

임제 선사의 온전한 기틀은 격조가 정말로 높고 높은지라,
주장자 머리 위에 눈이 있어서 가을철 털끝을 가림이로다.
야호와 토끼를 쓸어 없애니 가풍이 준걸함이요,
변화의 어룡을 번갯불에 사름이로다.

임제전기격조고(臨濟全機格調高)라

봉두유안변추호(棒頭有眼辨秋毫)로다.
소제호토가풍준(掃除狐兎家風峻)이요
변화어룡전화소(變化魚龍電火燒)로다.

사람을 살리는 칼과 사람을 죽이는 검이여!
하늘을 비껴 번쩍이니 날카로운 취모검이로다.
일등 영(令)을 행함은 그 맛이 특별함이니,
십분 아픈 곳을 이 누가 알리요.
도리어 임제 선사를 알겠는가?
아이고! 아이고! 곡을 함이로다.

활인도살인검(活人刀殺人劍)이여!
의천조설이취모(倚天照雪利吹毛)로다.
일등령행자미별(一等令行滋味別)이니
십분통처시수조(十分痛處是誰遭)오
환회임제마(還會臨濟麽)아?
창천 창천(蒼天 蒼天)이로다.

[주장자로 법상을 한 번 치시고 하좌하시다.]

총림대중들과 법회 참석을 위해 이동하시는 모습

Master Jinje on his way to give a Dharma teaching

Dialogue between Zhaozhou, Huangbo and Linji

End of the 2015 summer retreat at Donghwa-sa

[The Master ascends the Dharma Seat and shows the Dharma Staff to the assembly.]

Claim the Truth of this Dharma Staff, and

Your opportune condition is like securing arrows and swords.

You can distinguish between host and guest in a flash.

Don't claim the Truth of this Dharma Staff, but

The Staff has a luminous eye like the sun, and

You will manifest as a barbarian if a barbarian comes, and

Manifest as a civilian if a civilian comes.

Today marks the end of the three month summer retreat.

For those of you who have maintained the spirit and courage you had at the beginning of the retreat, and who have resolved the fundamental matter of life through perseverance, despite the intense summer heat, today will be the end of the retreat in its truest sense. However, for those of you who haven't, the end of this retreat only marks the beginning of a new retreat.

You should look into yourself again and again.

To truly end a retreat means to know your true nature by having broken through your *hwadu*, and to have become a person of great freedom who can travel the world without reservation. If not, you should brace your mind again and resolve to attain great enlightenment.

When you leave this monastery, you should neither wander from this mountain to that mountain in a hurry without mindfulness nor should you travel like a ghost with your *hwadu* stashed in your backpack.

It is impossible to attain the Great Way by passing time idly like that. You must realize that a retreat only truly ends when you shatter your *hwadu* and a virtuous master acknowledges your enlightenment. Until then, you should sit motionless like a rock, with an unwavering mind and practice again and again with all your might.

As you investigate your *hwadu*, every move you make and every step you take should arise from your heart, and you should keep your *hwadu* in mind with every step and every breath. You should strive diligently to maintain fervent doubt on your *hwadu* until it flows like a running river.

As you strive to attain one-pointed concentration on your *hwadu*, suddenly a true doubt will arise. Then you will become oblivious to sight, sound and even the passage of day and night. Days and months may pass in this condition until you suddenly break through your *hwadu*, perhaps merely upon seeing an object or hearing a sound. Then you can pierce hundreds or thousands of *gongan* (koan) of the Buddhas and Patriarchs as though with a single rod.

From that moment on, no matter what questions are thrown at you, you can give the right answer readily and stand shoulder to shoulder with all the Buddhas and Patriarchs.

At this level of attainment, you will enjoy the bliss of

enlightened concentration eternally, and even Old Yama can not take you to his realm of hell because you are invisible to him.

Once upon a time, Master Zhaozhou visited Master Huangbo during his wandering practice. Upon seeing Zhaozhou approach, Huangbo entered his own room and closed the door. Zhaozhou then walked into the Dharma hall and shouted,
"Fire! Fire!"
Then Huangbo came out, grabbed Zhaozhou and said,
"Speak! Speak!"
Huangbo answered, "You shot arrows after the thief ran away."

One day Master Zhaozhou visited Linji Monastery and was washing his feet when Master Linji came up and asked,
"What is the meaning of Bodhidharma coming from the west?"
Zhaozhou said, "As it happens, I am just now washing my feet."
Linji stepped up and leaned in closer, as if listening.
Zhaozhou said, "You should have known instantly. What is the use of ruminating?"

Then, Linji went away swinging his arms.

Zhaozhou said, "Today I put my feet in the wrong place for the first time in my thirty years of wandering practice."

Assembly! Do you know of Master Zhaozhou?

[The Master addresses the silent assembly.]

Master Zhaozhou
Attained the eye that penetrates from top to bottom.
Everywhere he went he met with virtuous teachers.
The One Phrase at the foundation of Truth shines eternally.

Assembly! Do you understand Master Huangbo?

A dragon and a tiger hit each other, and it is difficult to dodge the entire body.
Though it is the case
A good hand is offered to another good hand.
How many more examples like this can be found in the realms of heaven and humanity?

Assembly! Do you understand Master Linji?

The perfect attainment of Linji

Is truly noble and dignified.

His Dharma Staff has the eye that can discern

even the tiniest speck.

As he sweeps away tigers and rabbits,

his family tradition is superb.

He burns the sea dragon of change with lightning.

The sword that gives life and the blade that slays the living.

The flash against the blue sky tells us

It is the razor-sharp sword of Truth.

To perform a first-class order imparts special taste.

Who would recognize the spots of full pain?

Would you understand Master Linji?

Alas, Alas, I wail loudly.

[The Master hits the Dharma staff once and descends the Dharma Seat.]

불조심인전등 다례대재 법어
(佛祖心印傳燈 茶禮大齋 法語)

2015. 11. 5. 해운정사

불조심인 조사대전, 해운정사
Hall of Great Mind Seal of Buddha, Haeunjeong-sa

세간과 출세 간 진리의 세계, 어떤 것이 좋으냐?
봄이 되니 꽃이 피지 않는 곳이 없도다.

세여청산하자시(世與靑山何者是)냐?
춘성무처화불개(春成無處花不開)로다.

석가모니 부처님께서 세상에 나서시어 영산회상(靈山會上)에서 인천(人天) 백만 대중에게 꽃을 들어 보이시니, 마하가섭(摩訶迦葉)이 빙긋이 웃음에, 부처님의 깨달은 진리의 세계, 정법안장(正法眼藏) 열반묘심(涅槃妙心)을 마하가섭에게 전하시고, 부처님 열반하신 후 아난(阿難)이 가섭 존자께 묻되,

"부처님께서 발우와 금란가사 밖에 다른 법을 전하신 것이 있습니까?" 하니, "아난아, 문전의 찰간대를 거꾸러뜨려라" 하고 가섭 존자께서 대답하신지라. 아난 존자는 이 화두 법문(話頭法門)을 듣고 용맹정진하여 대오견성(大悟見性)하고, 가섭 존자의 정법안장(正法眼藏)을 받아 이어, 상나화수(商那和修)에게 전법(傳法)하심이로다.

대대손손 전하여 인도 28대 보리달마(菩提達磨) 존자에 이르니, 존자께서 동토(東土) 중국으로 건너오시어 교화하시다가 열반에 다다른 즈음 대중을 모아 놓고 "깨달은 바를 다 말해 보라. 진리에 계합(契合)하면 부처님의 심인법(心印法)을 전하리라"고 하시자,

신광(神光) 스님이 나와 삼배(三拜)를 하고 들어감에 "그대가 진리의 골수(骨髓)를 깨달았도다" 하시고 부처님의 심인법(心印法)을 혜가(慧可) 신광에게 전하시니, 이로 쫓아 중국에 선법(禪法)이 크게 흥함이로다.

하루는 임제 선사(臨濟禪師)께서 열반의 인연이 도래하여 제자 삼성(三聖) 스님을 불러, "네가 입을 열어 모든 사람을 어떻게 지도할라는고?" 라고 물으심에 삼성 스님이 문득 할(喝)을 하니, "불법이 저 눈먼 나귀에게 절단(切斷)됨을 누가 알리요?"라고 말씀하심이로다.

삼성 선사는 회상을 열지 않고 제방의 총림선원(叢林禪院)을 찾아 안거행각(安居行脚)을 하셨는데, 천오백 대중을 지도하고 계시는 위산영우(潙山靈佑) 선사 회상에 방부를 들여 대중과 함께 정진에 몰두하던 어느 날, 앙산(仰山) 선사가 삼성 선사를 마주 보자마자, "그대의 이름이 무엇인고?" 하고 물으니, "혜적(慧寂)입니다"라고 삼성 선사가 대답하거늘, 앙산 선사가 "혜적은 내 이름일세"라고 하자, 삼성 선사가 "예, 제 이름은 혜연(慧然)입니다"라고 함이라. 이렇게 자재(自在)하게 씀이 도인의 가풍이로다.

임제 선사의 문하에서 부처님의 심인법이 면밀히 전해져 석옥청공(石屋淸珙) 선사에 이름이라.

부처님의 선법(禪法)이 쇠퇴 일로를 걷고 있던 고려 말(末) 태고

보우(太古普愚) 스님이 중국 천지의 눈 밝은 선지식들로부터 부처님의 정법정안(正法正眼)을 전수받아 우리나라에도 바른 진리의 법을 펴야겠다는 큰 원(大願)을 세우고, 각고의 정진 끝에 뚜렷한 진리의 눈이 열리어 중국 땅에 들어감이라.

석옥 선사를 참방(參訪)하여 예배(禮拜)하고 말씀드리기를, "고려국에서 선사님의 고준하신 안목에 점검받으러 왔습니다"하니 석옥 선사께서 물음을 던지시기를, "우두법융(牛頭法融) 스님이 사조도신(四祖道信) 선사를 친견하기 전에는 어찌하여 천녀(天女)들이 공양을 지어 올리고, 온갖 새들이 꽃을 물어 왔는고?" 하고 물으시니, "부귀는 만인이 부러워합니다"라 답하고, "그렇다면 우두법융 스님이 사조 선사를 친견한 후로는 어찌하여 천녀들이 공양을 올리지도 않고 새들도 꽃을 물어 오지 아니했는고?"라는 물음에 "청빈은 모든 분에게 소외되기 쉽습니다"라고 답함이라.

석옥 선사께서 세 번째 물음을 던지시기를, "공겁(空劫) 전에 태고(太古)가 있었는가?"하시니, "공겁의 세계가 태고로 좇아 이루어졌습니다"라고 태고 스님이 답함에 "내가 일생토록 이 주장자를 써도 다 쓰지 못한 고로 이제 그대에게 부치노니, 잘 받아 가져서 광도중생(廣度衆生)하기 바라노라" 하시며 석옥 선사께서 주장자를 건네주시고, 부처님의 심인법을 부촉(咐囑)하심이로다.

태고 선사의 가풍이 면면히 이어져 내려와, 경허성우(鏡虛惺牛) 선사에 이르러 아손(兒孫)이 번성하니, 오늘날 세계 방방곡곡에 부처님의 진리의 선풍(禪風)을 널리 선양(宣揚)하여, 한국의 선법이 만방에 꽃을 피우고 있습니다.

필경(畢竟)에 가장 높은 진리의 한 마디는 어떠한 것인고?

한 주먹 버들가지 잡아 얻지 못해서
봄바람에 옥 난간 벽에다가 걸어 둠이로다.

일파유조수부득(一把柳條收不得)하야
화풍탑재옥난간(和風搭在玉欄干)이로다.

불기 2559년 음력 9월 24일

A Dharma Talk at the Great Memorial Ceremony for Buddhas and Patriarchs

2015 Memorial Ceremony at Haeunjeong-sa

Then, what is preferred?

The mundane or the supra-mundane?

All flowers bloom with the coming of spring.

Sakyamuni Buddha renounced the world and taught a hundred thousand beings and heavenly celestials by silently holding up a flower at the Vulture Peak assembly. When Mahakasyapa smiled, Buddha passed his teaching to him.

After Buddha entered parinirvana, Ananda enquired to Mahakasyapa, "Buddha transmitted to you a golden robe and the alms bowl of successorship. What other Dharma did he transmit?"

"Ananda! Knock down the flagpole at the gate!"

Mahakasyapa responded.

Upon hearing this *hwadu*, Ananda began a rigorous practice and attained great awakening. He received the treasury of the eye of true Dharma from Mahakasyapa, which was then transmitted to Sanakavasa.

Such profound Dharma were passed on from generation to generation up until Bodhidharma, the 28th Patriarch of Buddhism from India. Bodhidharma then passed on the great teachings to the eastern land of China. When he realized that his time on earth was drawing to an end, he called an assembly and said, "Each of you may demonstrate your understanding of Dharma. I will transmit the mind seal of Buddha to whoever can demonstrate true understanding."

Huike stepped forward and bowed deeply three times in silence and withdrew. Bodhidharma then said, "You have attained the marrow (essence) of the truth" and transmitted the mind seal of the Buddha to Huike, who then became guardian of truth that contributed greatly to the flourishing lineage of the Chinese Chan tradition.

When he was on his deathbed, Linji summoned Sangshen Huiran and asked him, "How do you plan to open those lips to teach the people?" When Huiran responded with a loud "Hal (roar)!" Linji said, "Who would have thought, that my true Dharma eye would be extinguished on reaching this blind donkey?"

Seon Master Huiran did not have an assembly of his own, but wandered the mountains from one great sangha assembly to another on a path of Seon pilgrimage and practice. One such assembly was given by Seon Master Weishan Lingyu and attended by over 1,500 mahasangha.

One day, when Master Yangshan Huiji was face to face with Master Sansheng Huiran he asked,
"What is your name?"
Master Huiran replied, "Huiji."
"That is my name." replied Master Huiji
Master Huiran responded, "Yes, my name is Huiran."

What a splendid manifestation of Dharma this was! A marvelous cultivation of Dharma on the path to enlightenment.

Thus, the mind seal of the Buddha was thoroughly transmitted from Master Linji to Master Shiyu.

Master Taego Bou, whose name literally means "time immemorial," aspired to start the lineage of authentic Dharma in Korea at a time when Buddhism was suffering a great decline. Hence, he practiced with strong effort and ultimately opened his eyes to the great Truth. In hopes of receiving the authentic Dharma of the Buddha, he traveled to China.

Master Taego Bou, when in audience with Seon Master Shiyu Quinggong (石屋淸珙) entreated him, "I braved the journey from Goryeo to learn the supreme Dharma from you."

Master Shiyu then tested him with the question, "What do you think of heavenly creatures and birds showering Master Niutou with gifts and flowers before his audience with the 4th Patriarch?"

"Everyone envies riches." Master Taego answered.

"Then, what do you think of the fact that the showering of gifts and flowers stopped after Master Niutou had an audience with the 4th Patriarch?"

"In poverty, even sons and daughters stay away."

Then the third question to Master Shiyu,

"Do the empty kalpas, in which no Buddha appears, come before time immemorial or after?"

Taego answered, "It abides in Taego."

Master Shiyu then conferred his seal of approval by giving Master Taego his Dharma staff and saying, "This staff has belonged to me my whole life, but I have not utilized it properly. Now, I am entrusting you with this Truth. You must guard it well so that illumination may flow unceasingly into the future."

Hence, Master Taego received the authentic Dharma of the Buddha until it reached the Great Seon Master Gyeongheo. The truth of BuddhaDharma was then exalted far and wide all over the world and Korean Seon blossomed in every direction.

What is the single word of truth in the highest Truth of Dharma?

Unable to grab a fistful of willows
Hang it on a jade fence in a spring breeze.

덕산 스님의 깨달음

2015.11.26. 을미년 동안거 결제 법어, 동화사

동화사 향곡대선사부도탑에서 금당선원 대중들과, 2015

Master jinje with practitioner at the stupa of Master Hyanggok, 2015

[상당하시어 주장자를 들어 대중에게 보이시고,]

흐르는 물에 배를 띄움은 오히려 쉬움이나
바람을 거슬러 키(柁)를 잡음은 세간에 드묾이라.
비록 이 좋은 담판한(擔板漢)이나
마침내 편의(便宜)에 떨어짐을 면치 못함이로다.
어떤 분이 이렇게 옴인고?

순수사선유자가(順水使船猶自可)어니와
역풍파타세간희(逆風把柁世間稀)라.
수연호개담판한(雖然好箇擔板漢)이나
도두미면낙편의(到頭未免落便宜)로다.
십마인 임마래(什麽人 恁麽來)오?

금일은 동안거 결제일이라.

이 삼동구순(三冬九旬)의 결제 기간 동안 대중들이 모여서 안거를 시작함은 부처님의 가르침인 생사해탈의 대오견성을 하기위한 것이다. 바람이 불고 비가 오는 성주괴공(成住壞空)의 이치처럼 인간도 나고 늙고 병들고 죽는 생로병사의 흐름 속에서 벗어나지 못하고 죽음에 이르러서야 세월의 흐름만 한탄하게 될 것이다.

세계에서 우리나라만큼 안거제도가 제대로 이어오고 있는 곳이 없으니 얼마나 다행한 일이며 얼마나 수행하기 좋은 곳인지 생각

한다면 부처님의 은혜와 시주의 은혜를 잊지 말고 일각(一刻)도 방일(放逸)하지 않아야 할 것이라.

이 몸은 100년 이내에 썩어서 한 줌 흙으로 돌아가 버리므로, 이 몸은 참다운 나가 아니다. 참다운 나가 어떤 것인지 모르는 까닭에 중생들은 나고 날 적마다 끝없는 고통의 바다에서 헤어날 수 없는 것이다.

그러니 화두가 있는 이는 각자의 화두를 챙기되, 화두가 없는 이는 '부모에게 나기 전에 어떤 것이 참나인가?' 이 화두를 일상생활 가운데에 앉으나 서나 가나 오나 일체처일체시(一切處一切時)에 놓치지 말고 챙겨야 할 것이다.

화두를 지어가는 사람은 부지기수임에도 어찌하여 일념삼매(一念三昧)를 지속하지 못하고 대오견성(大悟見性)을 하지 못하느냐? 중생은 낙동강 모래알의 숫자만큼이나 무한한 전생의 습기(習氣)가 태산같이 쌓여있기 때문이니, 반딧불 같은 신심과 용기로는 수천 생, 수만 생을 수행한다 해도 불가능하다. 그러니 모든 반연(攀緣)을 끊고 시비장단(是非長短)을 모두 내려놓고 견성하고 말겠다는 확고한 대신심(大信心)과 불타는 대용맹심(大勇猛心)을 내어 간절하게 마음에서 우러나오는 각자의 화두를 챙기고 의심하고 챙기고 의심하여 번뇌와 망상이 들어올 틈이 없도록 혼신의 노력을 쏟아야 함이로다.

그렇게 정성껏 잡도리하다 보면, 자기도 모르는 사이에 화두가 익어져서 밤낮으로 흐르고 흐르다가 문득 참의심이 발동하게 된다. 그때는 보는 것도 잊어버리고 듣는 것도 잊어버리고, 앉아있어도 밤이 지나가는지 낮이 지나가는지 며칠이 지나가는지 몇 달이 지나가는지 모르게 되니, 이것이 일념삼매(一念三昧)인 것이다.

이처럼 일념삼매가 시냇물이 끊어지지 않고 흐르는 것처럼 일주일이고 한 달이고 일 년이고 지속될 때, 홀연히 보는 찰나에 듣는 찰나에 화두가 박살나게 됨이로다. 그리하면 어떠한 법문에도 바른 답이 흉금(胸襟)에서 석화전광(石火電光)으로 흘러나와 여탈자재(與奪自在), 살활종탈(殺活縱奪)의 수완을 갖추고 억겁세월(億劫歲月)이 지나도록 진리의 낙을 수용하며 불조(佛祖)와 인천(人天)의 스승이 되어 천하를 종횡(縱橫)하는 대장부의 활개를 치게 됨이로다.

덕산(德山) 스님은 중국 북방지역 사찰에 거주하면서 일생 금강경을 독송하고 주(註)와 소(疎)로 일관한 스님이었다.

하루는 덕산 스님이 "남방 선지식들로부터 들려오는 말들이, '직지인심(直指人心) 견성성불(見性成佛)'이라, 곧 사람의 마음을 가리켜서 성품을 보고 부처를 이룸이라 하니, 이러한 말이 어찌 있을 수 있느냐? 내가 남방에 가서 모든 선지식들을 일봉(一棒)으로 때려서 벙어리가 되게끔 하리라."

굳게 다짐하고 북방을 출발하여 남방으로 향하였다. 여러 달을 걷고 걸어서 남방의 용담사(龍潭寺) 부근에 이르러, 점심때가 되어 요기를 하려고 사방을 살피던 중 노변에 빵을 구워 파는 노보살에게 다가갔다.

"점심 요기를 좀 합시다"

하니, 그 빵 굽는 노보살이 물었다.

"스님 바랑 속에 무엇이 그리 가득 들어 있소?"

"금강경 소초(疏秒)입니다."

그러니 노보살이 말하기를,

"내가 금강경의 한 대문(大文)을 물어서 답을 하시면 점심을 그냥 대접할 것이고, 만약 바른 답을 못하면 다른 데 가서 요기하십시오."

하니, 덕산 스님이 자신만만하게 물으라고 하였다. 노보살이 금강경 한 대문을 들어 묻기를

"금강경에 이르기를, '과거심(過去心)도 얻지 못하고, 현재심(現在心)도 얻지 못하고, 미래심(未來心)도 얻지 못한다' 하니, 스님은 과거심에다 점을 치시렵니까(點心), 현재심에다 점을 치시렵니까, 미래심에다 점을 치시렵니까?"

하니, 그 물음에 덕산 스님이 벙어리가 되어 답을 못하고 멍하게 서 있었다. 이에 노보살이 말하기를,

"바른 답을 못했으니 약속과 같이 다른 데 가서 요기하십시오. 그리고 10리쯤 올라가시면 용담사(龍潭寺)라는 큰 절이 있으니 용담(龍潭) 선사께 가서 불법을 물으십시오" 하였다.

그러면 이 보살은 어떤 보살이냐? 큰 용기와 신심으로 남방 마구니들을 한 방망이 때려서 벙어리로 만들겠다는 북방 덕산 스님의 그 용기와 큰 그릇됨(器)을 아시고 문수 보살이 빵 굽는 보살로 나투시어 접인(接引)한 것이다.

요기도 못하고 노보살에게 방망이를 맞고는 곧장 용담사를 찾아가 용담 선사 방문 앞에 이르러 말했다.

"용담이라 해서 찾아왔더니, 못(潭)도 보이지 않고 용(龍)도 나타나지 않는구나!"

하니, 용담 선사께서 그 말을 듣고 문을 열고 나오시면서

"그대가 친히 바로 용담(龍潭)에 이르렀네."

하고 방으로 맞으셨다. 밤이 늦도록 대담을 나누다가 덕산 스님이 객실로 가기 위해 방을 나오니, 밖이 칠흑같이 캄캄하여 한 걸음도 옮길 수가 없으므로 다시 방문을 열고는

"사방이 칠흑 같습니다. 불을 좀 주십시오."

함에 용담 선사께서 용심지에 불을 붙여 주니, 덕산 스님이 그것을 받는 순간 용담 선사께서 입으로 불어 불을 꺼버리셨다. 불을 끄는 찰나에 덕산 스님이 소리를 질러 말하기를

"이후로는 천하 도인의 언설(言說)을 의심하지 아니하리라."

하니, 거기서 크게 진리의 눈이 열린 것이다.

뒷날 아침에 용담 선사께서 대중방(大衆房)에 이르러 말씀하셨다.

"우리 대중 가운데 이빨은 칼날과 같고 입은 피를 담는 항아리와 같은 이가 있나니, 그가 몽둥이로 때리면 머리를 돌이키지 못하느

니라. 이후에 고봉정상(孤峰頂上)에서 나의 가풍의 도를 세워 가리
니, 시회대중(時會大衆)은 조심하고 조심하라!"

그런 후에 덕산 스님이 법당 앞뜰에서 금강경 소초에다 불을 댕
기면서 말하기를,

"모든 현현(玄玄)한 웅변으로써 진리의 법을 설한다 해도 털 한
가닥을 공중에 날리는 것과 같음이요, 세상의 모든 요긴한 기틀을
다하더라도 물 한 방울을 큰 골짜기에 던지는 것과 같음이라."

하고 금강경 소초를 불살라 버리고 용담 선사께 예배하고 떠났다.

시회대중은 덕산 선사를 알겠는가?

덕산 선사를 알기 위해서는 각자의 화두를 성성(惺惺)히 챙겨서
일념이 지속되는 과정이 와야 천불만조사(千佛萬祖師)와 더불어
동참하리니 모든 대중은 정진에 정진을 거듭할지어다.

필경에 덕산 선사를 알겠느냐?

[한참을 계시다 대중이 말이 없으니, 스스로 점검하여 이르시기를]

만 길이나 되는 높은 산봉우리에 앉아서
부처를 꾸짖고 조사를 꾸짖음이나
다리 아래 두 자, 석 자가 됨을 아느냐?

만인봉두좌(萬仞峯頭坐)하여

가불매조(呵佛罵祖)나

각하수삼척 회야마(脚下數三尺 會也麼)?

[주장자로 법상을 한 번 치시고 하좌하시다.]

Deshan's Awakening

Beginning of the 2015 winter retreat at Donghwa-sa Temple

금당선원에서 선원대중들과 - 동화사 대구, 2015

Master Jinje with practitioner from the Geumdang Seon Center, 2015

[The Master ascends the Dharma Seat and shows the Dharma Staff to the assembly.]

It is rather easy to set a ship afloat on a flowing river,
But steering against the wind is rare in the secular world.
Although this fine man carries a board across his shoulders,
Eventually he cannot avoid having some small convenience.
I wonder who is coming this way.

Today marks the beginning of the winter retreat.

For three winter months we come together to attain great enlightenment and see our true nature based on the Buddha's teachings, through which we will be liberated from birth and death. Otherwise, like the natural laws that follow the stages of formation, duration, destruction and emptiness, we humans won't escape the stages of birth, aging, sickness and death. Only at the moment of death, will we lament the swift passage of time.

Among all the nations of the world, no other nation has properly passed down the three-month summer and winter retreat system as Korea has. When you think of how fortunate you are and the favorable circumstance you have to do meditation practice, you must never get lazy even for a moment nor forget the kindness of the Buddha and our patrons.

As this body will return to the earth as a handful of dust in less than 100 years, this body is not my true self. Without knowing one's true self, sentient beings cannot escape the endless ocean of suffering they will encounter in every rebirth of their cyclic existence.

Therefore, keep to your *hwadu*, but if you do not have a *hwadu*, then accept the *hwadu* "What is your true self before you were born of your parents?" without ever losing focus of it, whether you are standing or sitting, coming or going. You must focus on it every waking moment, regardless of place and time.

Although a great number of practitioners investigate a *hwadu*, why is it that most of them cannot sustain one-pointed concentration and attain great awakening to see their true nature?

It is because in all their previous lives they have accumulated karmic impressions as numerous as the grains of sand in the River Ganges. With their faith and courage as feeble as the light of a firefly, they cannot be awakened even if they were to practice meditation for thousands or tens of thousands of lifetimes. You must cast aside all attachments and judgments of what is right or wrong. Then you must arouse great faith and great courage to investigate your *hwadu* and arouse fierce and earnest doubt from the depth of your heart without allowing any afflictions or delusions to enter your mind.

When you cultivate your practice sincerely and carefully in this way, your *hwadu* will ripen even without your awareness. Days and nights will pass while you are in this state of concentration, and suddenly true doubt will arise. Then you will forget to see or hear anything. You will lose track of time, and you will sit in meditation with no awareness of the passage of days or even months. That is true one-pointed concentration.

When you sustain this one-pointed concentration for a month or even a year without interruption, like a steadily flowing river, your *hwadu* will suddenly shatter the moment you see something or hear a sound. Then you can respond to any Dharma talk in a flash. You become skillful at giving and taking, in saving life and in taking life. You will embrace the joy of the Truth for limitless eons and become the teacher of Buddhas and Patriarchs, of humans and gods. You will spread Dharma far and wide with the unhindered freedom of great heroes.

Master Deshan resided in a temple in northern China. He

attained masterly knowledge of the Diamond Sutra by reciting it all his life, studying its commentaries, and lecturing about them.

One day, Deshan heard that the Southern School was teaching that by pointing directly to the human mind, one can see their true self-nature and attain Buddhahood. He uttered, "How dare they say such things! I will go there and confound all those Southern devils with a blow from my staff." And with firm resolve, he left for the South.

He walked several months and finally arrived in the vicinity of Longtansi (龍潭寺) Temple. As it was lunchtime he looked around for some food, and found an old woman selling bread by the roadside. He approached her and said, "Let me have some bread please!"

The old woman asked, "You seem to have a full backpack. What is in it?"

Deshan answered, "They are commentaries on the Diamond Sutra."

She then said, "I have a question for you about the Diamond Sutra. If you answer correctly, I will offer you lunch. If not, you'll have to go elsewhere."

Full of confidence, Deshan agreed.

The old woman said, "In the Diamond Sutra it says, 'The past mind is unattainable, the present mind is unattainable, and the future mind is unattainable.' Which mind do you aim to attain, the past mind, the present mind or the future mind?"

To this question Deshan was taken aback and just stood there dumbfounded without an answer.

Then the old woman said, "As you didn't respond, you should eat elsewhere. If you walk up the hill about 4 kilometers, there is a large temple called Longtansi. Ask Seon Master Longtan about the Buddha Dharma."

Who was this old woman? As Deshan was of the Northern School, he had resolved to hit the Southern devils with his staff to dumbfound them. Mañjuśrī Bodhisattva had recognized his courage and that he was a great vessel of the Dharma, so he had appeared as a bread-seller to guide Deshan.

Deshan, who was stung by the old woman's question and still hungry, went straight to Longtansi. Arriving at the door to Master Longtan's room, he said, "I've heard about the Dragon Pool [Longtan (龍潭) literally means "Dragon Pool"], but I see no pool, nor does the dragon appear."

Hearing this, Master Longtan opened the door and said, "You have truly arrived at the Dragon Pool," and invited Deshan into his room.

They talked extensively late into the night. When Deshan stepped outside to go to the guest room, it was too dark to see and he couldn't take even a single step. He opened the door to Longtan's room again and said, "It's pitch black outside. May I have a lamp?"

Master Longtan lit a lantern and held it out, but the moment Deshan received it, Master Longtan instantly blew it out.

The moment the light went out, Deshan cried out, "From now on I will never doubt the teaching of the venerable master."

His wisdom eye was opened at that moment.

The next morning, Master Longtan said to the assembly:

"In our community there is a practitioner who has teeth as sharp as a sword's blade, and a mouth like an earthen pot holding blood. When he hits you with his staff, you cannot turn your head. Later he will reside at the summit of a solitary peak and teach the Way in my tradition. Assembly at attendance! You must be careful, and then careful again."

Then Deshan piled up all his commentaries on the Diamond Sutra in front of the Dharma Hall, lifted a torch and said:

"All the teachings of truth, even when spoken in mysterious words, are like a single hair in a vast emptiness. All the affairs of the world, even performed with the essential capacity of understanding, are like a drop of water in a great mountain stream."

Deshan burned them all, paid his respects to Master Longtan and left.

Assembly present! Do you know Master Deshan?

In order to know him, you must investigate your *hwadu* in clarity and be able to sustain one-pointed concentration. Only then can you stand shoulder to shoulder with a thousand Buddhas and ten thousand Patriarchs. I exhort every one of you to keep exerting yourself in Seon meditation.

Do you know Master Deshan ultimately?

[The Master addresses the silent assembly.]

> Sitting atop a mountain peak 10,000 fathoms high
> He scolds Buddhas and rebukes Patriarchs.
> Does he know it is two or three feet long right under his feet?

[The Master hits the Dharma staff once and descends from the Dharma Seat.]

간화선, 최상승(最上乘)의 경절문(徑截門)

2013. 4. 24. 간화선 대법회 종정 법어, 조계사

대한불교조계종 종정 추대대법회(조계사, 2012)

Master Jinje at his installation ceremony as the Supreme Patriarch (Jongjeong) of the Jogye Order of Korean Buddhism held at Jogye-sa Temple (Seoul, 2012)

[상당하시어 주장자를 들어 대중에게 보이시고.]

한 생각 바로 앉아 찰나를 지나면
항하사 모래알 숫자와 같은 칠보탑을 조성하는 공덕을 지나감이라.
보배탑은 세월이 흘러 필경에는 흔적도 없거니와
한 생각 바른 신심은 바른 깨달음을 성취함이로다.

약인정좌일수유(若人靜坐一須臾)하면
승조항사칠보탑(勝造恒沙七寶塔)이라.
보탑필경화위진(寶塔畢竟化爲塵)어니와
일념정신변정각(一念正信便正覺)이로다.

부처님께서 깨달으신 가장 높은 진리의 도(道)가 중국으로 와서 크게 흥하다가 한국으로 건너왔는데, 지금은 오직 우리나라에만 한 줄기 남아 있습니다. 부처님께서 중생들의 근기에 따라 가지가지의 명상법과 가지가지의 수행법을 베풀어주셨지만, 최상승(最上乘) 수행법인 견성법(見性法)만큼은 뭇 중생들이 알아가지질 못하였습니다.

그러나 다행히도 오직 가섭존자만이 견성법을 얻어 부처님과 이심전심(以心傳心)하니, 비로소 부처님의 심인법(心印法)이 가섭, 아난으로 좇아 제 28조 달마대사에 이르러 중국으로 건너와 지금은 단 한 가닥 한국에 내려오고 있습니다.

역대의 모든 불조(佛祖)께서 심인법이 끊어지지 않도록 노심초사 간절하게 견성법을 지도하였는데 2,500여 년이 지난 오늘날까지도 이렇게 한국의 선불장(選佛場)에서 재현되고 있으니 이 얼마나 다행스러운 일인지 모릅니다.

그런데 요즘 들어 부처님께서 근기에 맞추어 가르치는 데 불과했던 관법(觀法)수행이 선원 내에서도 유포된다 하니 안타까운 마음입니다. 이 견성법은 모든 근기를 아우르는 수행법이요, 일체의 다른 방편을 구하지 않고 바로 여래지(如來地)에 이르는 경절문(徑截門)이며, 눈 밝은 선지식을 만나 바르게만 지도받는다면 한 생에 다해 마칠 수 있는 참선수행법입니다.

혹자는 이러한 간화선(看話禪) 견성법이 중국에서 만들어졌다고 말하지만, 실은 부처님께서 간화선이라는 표현을 쓰시지 않으셨을 뿐입니다. 부처님께서도 일생토록 '어떻게 하면 생로병사에서 벗어나겠는가?'하는 간절한 의심 하나로 6년간 삼매(三昧)에 드셨는데 새가 머리에 집을 지어도 모르셨습니다.

그러다가 그동안 배우고 닦아왔던 모든 수행법을 내려놓고 마지막 일주일 동안은 오로지 일생토록 의심해왔던 '생로병사 해탈'의 깊은 의심삼매에 들어 있다가, 새벽녘에 홀연히 동쪽 하늘에 샛별이 반짝이는 것을 보시고 대오견성(大悟見性) 하셨습니다. 이것이 바로 간화선 견성법입니다. 이후로도 부처님께서는 '염화미소(拈花微笑)', '다자탑전반분좌(多子塔前半分座)', '곽시쌍부(槨示雙趺)'의 삼처전심(三處傳心)'을 통해 최상승의 진리의 세계를 열어 보이셨고, 이러한 견성법으로 법을 전하신 것입니다.

　그러니 모든 분이 이 같은 '참선대법회'를 통해 간화선의 가치를 제대로 알고 바르게 참선지도를 받아 진실되게 참구하시기 바랍니다.

　그러면 어떻게 닦는 것이 바른 참선수행법인가? 화두가 있는 이는 각자 화두를 참구하시고 화두가 없는 이는
　"부모에게 나기 전에 어떤 것이 참나인가?"
　이 화두를 일상생활 속에서 마음에서 우러나오는 간절한 마음으로 오매불망 의심하는 것입니다. 이 몸뚱이는 숨 한 번 들이마시고 내쉬지 못하면 바로 다음 생이라, 생과 사가 마치 옷 갈아입는 것과 같아서 참나라고 할 수 없으니 영원토록 변치 않는 참나를 찾아야 합니다. 그러니 일상생활하는 가운데 하루에도 천 번 만 번 "부모에게 나기 전에 어떤 것이 참나인가?"하고 끊임없이 화두를 챙기고 의심을 밀어주어야 합니다.

　이렇게 끊임없이 화두를 챙기고 의심을 밀어주라는 이유는, 촌의 방앗간에서 방아 찧는 기계가 한 번 시동이 걸리면 하루 종일 방아를 돌릴 수 있는 것과 마찬가지로, 무한한 노력 가운데 문득 참의심이 시동 걸리게 하기 위해서입니다.

　그렇게 화두 한 생각이 시동이 걸리면 그때는 흐르는 시냇물처럼 끊어짐 없이 화두의심이 흘러갑니다. 그러면 사물이 보여도 보는 감각이 없고 소리가 들려도 듣는 감각이 없어서 마치 목석과 같

은 바보가 되어 버립니다.

그렇게 간절한 화두의심 한 생각으로 마치 바보처럼 보고 듣는 것이 다 마비되어 한 달이고 일 년이고 십 년이고 시간이 흐르고 흐르다가, 홀연히 사물을 보고 소리를 듣는 찰나에 화두가 박살이 나면서 자기의 참성품을 보게 되는 것입니다. 그러면 한 걸음도 옮기지 않고 부처님 땅에 이르러 너도 장부(丈夫)요 나도 부처가 되어 모든 불조와 어깨를 나란히 하게 되는 것입니다. 이것을 일러 견성이라고 합니다.

모든 부처님과 조사스님들께서 바로 이러한 심심미묘(甚深微妙)한 견성법을 전하고 전하신 것이며, 그 견성법이 오직 한 가닥 이곳 한국에 머물러 있는 것입니다. 그러니 우리가 얼마나 복된 인연으로 이토록 귀한 견성법을 만났는가를 알아 소소한 마음 챙기는 수행법에 눈 돌리지 말고, 세세생생 만나기 힘든 인간 몸 만났으니 이번 생은 태어나지 않은 셈치고 부처님의 대도를 이루겠다는 작심을 하고 정진에 임해야 하겠습니다.

그러면 간화선 바른 수행법의 좋은 예로 산승의 구도(求道)의 과정을 말씀드릴까 합니다.

산승은 경남 남해에서 태어나 자랐는데 절에 자주 다니던 친척 어른을 따라서, 동네에서 10리쯤 떨어진 곳에 있던 해관암이라는 조그마한 사찰에 갔다가, 석우(石友) 선사를 친견(親見)한 것이 출가의 인연이 되었습니다.

당시 석우 선사는 승속을 막론하고 당대에 가장 존경받는 선승이셨고, 대도인으로 명성이 자자했던 분이셨습니다. 그래서 해제 철만 되면 제방에서 정진하던 스님네들이 한 철 공부를 점검받기 위해 그 먼 남해섬까지 석우 선사를 찾아왔습니다.

석우 선사께서 산승을 보시더니 곧장 물으셨습니다.

"세상의 생활도 좋지만 그보다 더 값진 삶이 있으니, 네가 한번 해보지 않겠느냐?"

"무엇이 그리 값진 삶입니까?"

"범부(凡夫)가 위대한 부처 되는 법이 있으니, 이 세상에 태어나지 않은 셈 치고 그 법을 구해보지 않겠느냐?"

선사님의 그 말씀에 왠지 모르게 마음이 끌리게 되었습니다. 그래서 수행하는 스님들의 생활을 유심히 살펴보니, 세상에서는 볼 수 없었던 청정한 생활 속에 수행하며 사는 것을 알게 되었습니다. 큰 환희심이 우러나오면서 결심을 하고 부모님께 허락을 얻어 출가하여 행자 생활을 시작했습니다. 선사님 시봉에다 공양주 소임, 땔감을 구해오고, 채소를 가꾸는 등 해야 할 일들이 연속이었습니다.

그러다가 석우 선사께서 해인사 조실로 추대되심에 모시고 가서 시봉하다가 그 해 사미계를 받았습니다. 그런 후로 조계종 초대 종정(宗正)으로 추대되시니, 동화사로 거처를 옮기어 종정 스님 시자로 공양주를 하면서 다시 모셨습니다.

섣달 그믐날 대중들이 팔공산 정상으로 등산하러 간다기에 따라 나서게 되었습니다. 내려오는 길에 어떤 스님이 정진하던 토굴이 하나 있었는데, 토굴이 비어 있고 양식도 좀 있어 같이 간 대중 몇 사람이 "우리가 여기에서 일주일 용맹정진(勇猛精進)을 하자"는 의견을 내놓았습니다. 그러자 다들 그 자리에서 용맹정진 발심이 일어나 일주일간 지내다 내려왔습니다.

그런데, 어른 시봉한다는 사람이 노스님께 말씀도 드리지 않고 허락도 없이 일주일간 토굴에서 용맹정진을 하다 왔으니, 석우 선사께서는 "어른이 시키는 대로 하지 않고 제멋대로 온갖 것을 다 하려고 한다"고 호통을 치셨습니다. 그러나 선사께서는 저의 참학 의지를 아시고 '부모미생전본래면목(父母未生前本來面目)' 화두를 주셨습니다.

그 후 산승이 스물 넷 되던 해(1957년) 강원을 마치고 여름 해제 후, 종정 스님의 허락을 얻어 걸망을 짊어지고 선문(禪門)에 들어 운수행각(雲水行脚)의 길에 올랐습니다. 첫 행선지가 태백산 각화사 동암이었는데 당시에는 모두 비어 있었습니다. 동암에 가니 자잘한 피감자가 가마니에 덮여 있어서 감자를 양식으로 삼고는 혼자서 모든 반연(攀緣)을 끊고 밤낮으로 정진에만 몰두했습니다.

그렇게 혼자 두 달을 지내는데, 어느 날 도반이 각화사 주지를 맡게 되어 올라와서는 끼니가 변변찮은 것을 걱정하며 함께 내려가서 살자고 자꾸 청하는 바람에, 같이 있다가는 공부가 안되겠다 싶어 바랑을 싸서는 선산 도리사로 갔습니다.

도리사에서 일고여덟 분의 수좌(首座) 스님들과 동안거를 나게 되었는데, 밤 아홉 시가 되어 방선(放禪)하면 잠시 누웠다가 모두 잠든 후에 조용히 일어나 두세 시간 포행정진하며 하루하루를 빈틈없이 정진하였습니다.

그러던 어느 날 참선 도중에 반짝 떠오르는 조그마한 지견(知見)을 가지고서 '알았다'는 잘못된 소견을 갖게 되었습니다. 참구하던 것을 다 놓아 버리고는 해제일만 기다렸는데, 그러던 중 은사 스님이시고 초대 종정이신 석우 선사께서 열반에 드셨다는 부고가 날아와 동화사로 가서 다비(茶毘)를 치렀습니다.

그런 후에 당시에 대도인으로 명성이 자자했던, 경남 월내 묘관음사에 주석하고 계시던 향곡(香谷) 선사를 찾아갔습니다.

찾아가니 향곡 선사께서 대뜸 물으시기를,

"일러도 삼십 방(三十棒)이요, 이르지 못해도 삼십 방이니 어떻게 하려느냐?" 하셨습니다. 산승이 말을 못 하고 우물쭈물하자, 향곡 선사께서 '남전참묘(南泉斬猫)' 법문을 들어 다시 물으셨습니다.

옛날 남전(南泉) 선사 회상에 700명 대중이 모여서 참선 정진을 하던 때에 절에 고양이가 한 마리 있었다. 법당을 기준으로 동쪽 선방에서 참선하는 스님들은 그 고양이를 동쪽 선방 고양이라 하고, 서쪽 선방에서 참선하는 스님들은 그 고양이를 서쪽 선방 고양이라 해서 시비가 자주 일었다.

남전 선사께서 그 광경을 보시고는 시자를 불러 운집종을 치라 하시니, 대중이 하던 일을 모두 멈추고 법당에 모여들었다. 남전 선사께서 법상에 올라 시자에게 명하시었다.

"시자야, 고양이를 잡아오고, 칼도 가져오너라."

시자가 고양이와 칼을 남전 선사에게 올리니, 남전 선사께서 고양이를 들고 말씀하셨다.

"동쪽 선방에서 참선하는 스님들은 이 고양이를 동쪽 선방 고양이라 하고, 서쪽 선방에서 참선하는 스님들은 서쪽 선방 고양이라 하니, 지금 이 고양이에 대해서 분명히 한 마디 이르는 자가 있으면 고양이를 살려두거니와 만약 바른 답을 못하면 이 고양이를 두 동강 내리라."

700명 대중이 '내 고양이, 네 고양이'만 했지 남전 선사가 고양이를 들고 이르라는 뜻을 아무도 몰랐다. 대중이 답을 못하니 남전 선사께서는 약속대로 칼로 고양이를 두 동강이 내서 던져버렸다. 그리고는 조실방으로 가서 쉬고 있는데, 아끼는 제자 조주(趙州) 스님이 밖에 소임이 있어 나갔다가 돌아와서 인사를 올리니, 남전 선사께서

"오늘 대중에게 고양이 법문이 있었는데, 그대가 만약 그 자리에 있었다면, 고양이를 들고 이르라고 할 때에 뭐라고 답을 한마디 하겠느냐?"

하시니, 조주 스님이 신발을 머리에 이고 밖으로 나가버렸다. 이것을 보고 남전 선사께서 말씀하셨다.

"그대가 만약 그 대중 가운데 있었더라면, 고양이를 살릴 수 있었을텐데."

향곡 선사께서 산승에게
"남전 선사의 참묘법문 가운데 조주 선사께서 신발을 머리에 이고 나가신 것에 대해서 한마디 일러 보아라."
하고 물으셨는데, 산승은 여기서도 바른 답을 하지 못하였습니다. '알았다'고 자신만만해 있었는데 그만 여지없이 방망이를 맞은 것입니다. 그렇지만 당시에는 산승이 선지식(善知識)에 대한 믿음이 정립되어 있지 않았던 때라, '알았다'는 생각을 쉽게 놓아 버릴 수가 없었습니다. 그래서 제방을 행각하면서 당시 선지식으로 유명하였던 고승들을 거의 다 참방하면서 2년 여 시간을 허비하게 되었습니다.

세월을 그렇게 보내다가 스물여섯 때 오대산 상원사(上院寺)에서 일고여덟 명 선객 스님들과 동안거를 지내게 되었습니다.

생활은 얼마나 궁핍했던지, 좌복 하나를 가지고 정진할 때는 좌복으로 쓰고 잘 때는 배를 덮고 잤습니다. 먹는 것도 겨울철에 딱 한 번 두부를 울력해서 만들어 먹었을 뿐, 석 달을 배추김치 하나로 지냈습니다. 과일도 얼마나 귀했던지, 원주(院主) 스님이 하루는 어디를 다녀오면서 사과를 구해 왔는데, 석 달 동안 한 개 반씩만 나눠 먹을 정도였습니다. 춥기는 또 얼마나 추운지, 숭늉을 방에 떠 놓으면 숭늉이 얼 정도였고, 눈이 오면 처마 밑까지 쌓였습니다. 이처럼 지금은 상상하기 어려울 정도로 아주 힘들게 공부했습니다.

그렇게 정진을 하던 중, 유달리 포근한 날이 있어 남쪽 마루에 앉아 문득 자신을 반조(反照)해 보게 되었습니다. '내가 정말로 견성을 했느냐? 견성을 했으면 일일법문(一一法問)에 전광석화와 같이 즉시 바른 답이 나와야 하거늘 왜 그렇지 못하는가? 내가 나를 속여서야 되겠느냐! 이것은 큰 잘못됨이 있으니 내가 이 소견을 가지고 만족을 한다면 아무 쓸 곳이 없다. 백지 상태에서 다시 출발해야겠다. 나를 속이고 모든 이를 속이면 죄가 이만저만 아니다' 생각하고 스스로 반성하게 되었습니다.

이렇게 '알았다'하는 잘못된 소견을 놓아버리고 다시 공부를 시작하리라는 결심을 세우자 이전과 같은 오류에 빠지지 않기 위해서는 반드시 눈 밝은 선지식을 의지하여 공부해야만 한다는 인식을 분명히 갖게 되었습니다.

그러니 문답 과정에서 언하(言下)에 '옳다, 그르다' 칼질하셨던 향곡 선사 한 분에게만 확고한 믿음이 서게 되었습니다. 그래서 해제하자마자 향곡 선사 회상(會上)을 찾아갔습니다. 그리하여 향곡 선사께 예를 올리고,

"이 일을 마칠 때까지 스님을 의지해서 공부하려고 왔습니다. 화두를 하나 내려주십시오."

하고 말씀드리니, 향곡 선사께서

"이 어려운 관문을 네가 어찌 해결할 수 있겠느냐? 못한다!"

하시기에 분명히 선을 그어 말씀드렸습니다.

"신명을 다 바쳐서 해보겠습니다. 이 관문을 뚫기 전에는 절대 바랑 지고 산문(山門)을 나가지 않겠습니다."

이렇게 굳은 의지를 보여드리니, 그제서야 향곡 선사께서 '향엄상수화(香嚴上樹話)' 화두를 하나 내려주셨습니다.

"어떤 사람이 아주 높은 나무 위에서 손으로 가지를 잡거나 발로 가지를 밟지도 않고 입으로만 나뭇가지를 물고 매달려 있을 때, 나무 밑에서 지나가는 이가 달마 스님이 서역에서 중국으로 오신 뜻(祖師西來意)을 묻는데 있어서 대답하지 않으면 묻는 이의 뜻에 어긋나고, 만약 대답한다면 수십 길 낭떠러지에 떨어져서 자기 목숨을 잃게 될 것이다. 이러한 때를 당하여 어찌해야 하겠느냐?"

그리하여 이 화두를 들고 2년여 동안 생사를 떼어 놓고 공부하였습니다. 드디어 스물여덟 가을, 새벽에 예불 드리러 법당으로 올라가다가 마당의 돌부리에 걸려 넘어져 일어나는 차제(此際)에 화두가 박살이 났습니다. 그동안 동문서답하던 것이 다 해결된 것입니다. 그때야 맛을 알았습니다. 종전에 안 것은 아무것도 아니었습니다. 그래서 게송을 지어 바치기를,

이 주장자 이 진리를 몇 사람이나 알꼬?
과거, 현재, 미래의 모든 부처님도 다 알지 못함이로다.
한 막대기 주장자가 문득 금빛 용이 되어서

한량없는 용의 조화를 마음대로 부림이로다.

자개주장기인회(這箇拄杖幾人會)아
삼세제불총불식(三世諸佛總不識)이라.
일조주장화금룡(一條拄杖化金龍)어니
응화무변임자재(應化無邊任自在)로다.

하니, 향곡 선사께서 보시고는 앞 글귀는 묻지 아니하고 뒤 글귀를 잡아서 물으시기를,
"너 문득 용 잡아먹는 금시조를 만난다면 어떻게 하겠느냐?"
하셨습니다. 이에 산승이
"몸을 움츠리고 당황해서 세 걸음 물러가겠습니다(屈節當胸退身三步)."
라고 말씀드리니,
"옳고, 옳다."
하시며 크게 기뻐하셨습니다.
그런데 이렇게 '향엄상수화'를 깨달은 후에 향곡 선사와 문답하던 중, 유일하게 막힌 대문(大文)이 하나 있었습니다.

당나라 때 대선지식이셨던 마조(馬祖) 선사께서 열반하기 직전에 편찮으셨는데, 원주(院主)가 아침에 문안을 드리며,
"밤새 존후(尊候)가 어떠하셨습니까?" 하니, 마조 선사께서

"일면불월면불(日面佛月面佛)이니라" 하셨다.

'밤새 존후가 어떠하셨습니까?'라는 문안에 마조 선사께서는 왜 '일면불월면불'이라며 두 부처님의 이름을 말하셨을까? 이 화두는 가장 알기가 어려운 고준한 법문입니다. 마조 선사는 문하에 84명의 뛰어난 도인 제자를 두신 역대 선지식들께서도 부처님 이후 가장 위대한 도인이라 평하는 분입니다. 이 '일면불월면불' 말씀에는 마조 선사의 모든 살림살이가 다 들어 있습니다. 그래서 마조 선사를 바로 알려면 이 법문을 알아야만 합니다.

산승도 여기에 막혀서 거의 5년 동안 신고(辛苦)를 했는데, 자나 깨나 화두의심 한 생각밖에 없었습니다. 예나 지금이나 묘관음사에는 눈 오는 때가 거의 없는데, 하루는 음력 정월 아침에 일어나서 방문을 열고 나오니 온 산에 눈이 자욱하게 쌓여 있었습니다. 그런데 물을 가득 담아 놓았던 마당의 큰 통에는 눈이 다 녹아서 한 송이도 없었습니다. 그 물을 보는 찰나에 화두가 박살이 나니, 마침내 고인(古人)들께서 중중으로 베풀어놓으신 온갖 차별법문(差別法門)이 하나도 걸림 없이 회통이 되었습니다. 그래서 게송을 지어 올리기를,

한 몽둥이 휘둘러 비로정상을 거꾸러뜨리고
벽력 같은 일 할로써 천만 갈등을 문대버림이로다.
두 칸 띠암자에 다리 펴고 누웠으니
바다 위 맑은 바람 만년토록 새롭도다.

일봉타도비로정(一棒打倒毘盧頂)하고
일할말각천만측(一喝抹却千萬則)이라.
이간모암신각와(二間茅庵伸脚臥)하니
해상청풍만고신(海上淸風萬古新)이로다.

이렇게 올리니, 향곡 선사께서 "부처님의 마음법을 전해 받은 육조, 마조, 임제의 가풍이 이 글 속에 다 있구나!"하시며 "네 대(代)에 선풍이 만방에 드날리리라!"하고 극찬을 하셨습니다.

그 후 정미년 하안거 해제법회일에 묘관음사 법당에서 향곡 선사께서 법문을 하시기 위해 법상에 오르셔서 좌정하시고 계시는 차제에, 산승이 나아가서 예삼배(禮三拜)를 올리고 여쭈었습니다.
"불조(佛祖)께서 아신 곳은 여쭙지 아니하거니와, 불조께서 아시지 못한 곳을 일러 주십시오."
"구구는 팔십일이니라."
"그것은 불조께서 다 아신 곳입니다."
"육육은 삼십육이니라."
이에 산승이 아무 말 없이 선사께 예배드리고 물러가니, 향곡 선사께서도 아무 말 없이 법상에서 내려오셔서 조실방으로 돌아가셨습니다.
뒷날 조실방을 찾아가서 예를 갖추고 다시 여쭈었습니다.
"불안(佛眼)과 혜안(慧眼)은 여쭙지 아니하거니와, 어떤 것이 납승(衲僧)의 안목입니까?"

"비구니 노릇은 원래 여자가 하는 것이니라(師姑元來女人做)."

"금일에야 비로소 선사님을 친견하였습니다."

이에 향곡선사께서 물으셨습니다.

"네가 어느 곳에서 나를 보았는고?"

"관(關)!"

산승이 이렇게 답하자, 향곡 선사께서

"옳고, 옳다!"하시며, 임제정맥(臨濟正脈)의 법등(法燈)을 부촉(付囑)하시고 '진제(眞際)'라는 법호와 함께 전법게(傳法偈)를 내리셨습니다. 이때가 1967년, 산승의 나이 서른셋 되던 해였습니다.
[부처님으로부터 내려오는 제79대 법손]

진제법원 장실에 부치노니,

부처님과 도인의 산 진리는

전할 수도 없고 또한 받을 수도 없나니

이제 그대에게 산 진리를 전하노니

만인 앞에 진리의 전(廛)을 펴거나 거두거나 그대에게 맡기노라.

부 진제법원 장실(付 眞際法遠 丈室)

불조대활구(佛祖大活句)는

무전역무수(無傳亦無受)라.

금부활구시(今付活句時)에

수방임자재(收放任自在)로다.

산승이 도를 이루고 나서 살펴보니 부처님의 최고의 진리를 깨닫기 위해서는 간화선 수행법이 아니고서는 도저히 불가능하다는 것을 알았습니다. 불가에는 기도, 염불, 주력, 비파사나 관법수행 등 여러 가지 수행법이 있지만 다들 다겁생으로 무한토록 닦아야 하는 근기에 따른 수행일 뿐, 부처님께서 가섭에게 전하여 내려온 최상의 수행법이 아님을 알아야 합니다.

역대의 모든 조사 스님들께서 참선법만을 선양하신 데에는 뜻이 있는 것이며, 조계종의 종지종풍(宗旨宗風)이 이와 맥을 같이 하는 것입니다. 부처님의 간화선 수행법, 즉 참선 수행법은 한 걸음도 옮기지 않고 부처님의 땅에 이르는 지름길이 되는 수행법이며, 이 수행법을 통해 불조의 법맥이 내려오고 있는 것입니다. 그렇다고 참선 수행법이 결코 절집 스님네만의 전유물이 아닙니다. 꿀이 달고 소금이 짠 것을 안다면 누구나 닦을 수 있고 반드시 닦아야 할 수행법입니다.

세계는 지금 문화의 시대에 들어섰고, 이미 서구의 지성인들과 종교지도자들은 마음의 평안과 지혜로운 삶을 얻기 위해 종교를 떠나 마음 닦는 수행을 생활화하고 있으며, 정신수행을 가장 중요한 삶의 덕목으로 여기고 있습니다. 그들은 또한 어떠한 국가나 종교나 힘으로도 참다운 세계 평화와 인류의 행복한 미래를 만들어

낼 수 없으며, 오직 인류 개개인의 마음 수양과 정신고양만이 바른 해법이라고 말하고 있습니다. 나아가 세계는 종교와 국가를 초월하여 21세기 인류의 밝은 미래를 이끌어갈 정신문화로 우리의 간화선에 주목하고 있습니다.

그러므로 대중 여러분, 이젠 모든 분이 종교를 초월하여 참선 수행으로 마음을 닦아서 진리를 깨달아 진정한 평화를 얻어야 합니다. 그간 우리가 불우한 이웃을 돕는 일을 우선했다면, 이제는 한 걸음 더 나아가 자랑스러운 우리의 정신문화인 참선 수행법을 하루빨리 세계화하는 데 주력하여 참된 세계 평화와 인류의 행복에 기여하도록 합시다. 그래서 만인의 지혜가 더욱 증장되고, 우리의 이상인 정토세계와 극락세계가 이 지구촌에 이루어지기를 간절히 바랍니다.

산승의 스승인 향곡 선사께서 열반 일주일 전에 제방의 조실 스님들을 찾아다니며 '임제탁발화(臨濟托鉢話)' 법문을 들어 물으셨습니다.

임제 선사께서 하루는 발우를 가지고 탁발을 나가셨는데, 한 집에 가서 대문을 두드리니, 노보살이 대문을 열고 나오더니 임제 선사를 보고는 대뜸
"염치없는 중이로구나!"
하고는 한 푼의 시주도 하지 않았다. 그래서 임제 선사께서,
"어째서 한 푼 시주도 하지 않고 염치없는 중이라 하는고?"

물으시니, 노보살이 대문을 왈칵 닫고는 집 안으로 들어가 버렸다. 이에 임제 선사께서는 아무 말 없이 절로 돌아가셨다.

이 법문을 가지고 제방의 조실 스님들을 일일이 찾아다니며 물으셨는데, 모두들 흡족한 답을 내놓지 못하신 것이었습니다. 그래서 제방을 다 돌고 해운정사로 산승을 찾아오셨는데, 때마침 제가 마당에서 포행을 하고 있었습니다. 선사께서 산승을 보자마자, 들어가서 인사받고 물으셔도 될 터인데 얼마나 답답하셨는지,

"네가 만약 당시에 임제 선사가 되었던들 무엇이라고 한마디 하겠느냐?"

하시며 마당에 들어선 채로 산승에게 물으셨습니다. 이에 산승이 물음이 채 끝나기도 전에 척 답을 드리니,

"과연 나의 제자로다!"

하시며 그때서야 종전의 모습을 거두고 파안대소(破顔大笑)를 하셨습니다.

그러면 모든 대중 여러분, 당시에 임제 선사였다면 무엇이라고 한마디 하시겠습니까?

**삼십여 년간 말을 타고 희롱해 왔더니
금일 당나귀에게 크게 받힘을 입음이로다.**

삼십년래농마기(三十年來弄馬騎)러니

금일각피려자박(今日却被驢子搏)이로다.

석일(昔日)에 여덟 살 여식 아이가 말을 못한 것을 보시고, 두 분의 유명한 선지식께서 말씀하셨습니다. 한 분은 여식 아이가 여덟 살까지 말을 못한 것은 대도(大道)의 진리를 온전히 든 것이라 하시고, 또 한 분은 여덟 살의 여식 아이가 말을 못한 것은 대도의 진리를 듣기가 어려워서 말을 못한 것이라 하셨습니다.

대중이여, 두 분 선지식의 고견에 대해 어느 분이 멋진 답을 하셨습니까. 두 분의 답 중에 어느 것이 옳다고 보십니까?

[대중이 말이 없으니 이르시기를]

동지와 한식일은 백오일(百五日)이로다.

모든 국민이여,
남과 북이 무장으로 대치하고 경제 또한 어려운 이 시기에, 모든 분이 각자의 직분에 충실하다면, 경제와 국방이 더욱 견실해져서 하루빨리 이 난국을 헤쳐나갈 것이며, 남북의 평화통일은 성큼 다가올 것입니다.

나아가 모든 분이 일상생활하는 그 가운데 하루에도 천 번 만 번

"부모에게 나기 전에 어떤 것이 참나인가?"하고 간절하게 참나를 찾아서, 나고 날 적마다 큰 지혜를 얻어 무량한 행복을 누리소서.

[주장자로 법상을 한 번 치고 하좌하시다.]

장군죽비를 들고 정진대중들을 경책하시는 모습(동화사 금당선원)

Master Jinje training the practitioners with a bamboo clapper at the Geumdang Seon Center

조계사에서 열린 종정 추대 법회의 청법(請法) 대중, 2012

The Supreme Patriarch Installation Ceremony held at Jogye-sa Temple (Seoul, 2012)

Ganhwa Seon,
the Supreme Path to Enlightenment

April 24, 2013, at Jogye-sa

[The Master ascends the Dharma Seat and shows the Dharma Staff to the assembly.]

> **A moment passes sitting in practice focused on a single thought,**
> **One accrues merits surpassing erecting countless bejeweled stupas**
> **Bejeweled stupas will surely vanish in time without a trace**
> **But a single-focused mind and right faith will bear enlightenment.**

The highest path to Truth that the Buddha awakened to was transmitted to China, where it flourished greatly before being introduced to Korea. At present, this path only exists in Korea. The Buddha taught diverse methods of meditation and various practices of mind cultivation tailored to the needs of people with different levels of ability and attainment. However, the Dharma of seeing the true nature of mind, the supreme practice, was not attained by many. Fortunately, Ven. Mahakasyapa alone attained the Dharma of seeing one's true nature through mind-to-mind transmission from the Buddha. This Dharma of the mind seal of the Buddha was passed on to Mahakasyapa and to Ananda, and when the lineage passed on to the 28th Patriarch Bodhidharma, this Dharma was introduced to China. At present only a single lineage is being passed on in Korea.

All generations of Buddhas and Patriarchs preserved the Dharma of the mind seal with fervent devotion so that it wouldn't be disrupted or discontinued. It is truly fortunate that after 2,500 years, this Dharma is still vibrantly taught and practiced in Korea's Seon monasteries. It is regrettable that Vipassana meditation, which the Buddha applied to a specific group of people only to accommodate their capacity, is practiced in Korean Seon monasteries. However, the Dharma of seeing one's true nature can be practiced universally by anyone regardless of their capacity. It is a direct path and shortcut to attaining Buddhahood that does not require any other expedient means. If you are fortunate enough to receive correct guidance from an enlightened teacher, you may even attain enlightenment in this lifetime through this Seon practice.

Some people say this Dharma of seeing one's true nature, called "Ganhwa Seon," was developed in China, but in fact, it was taught by the Buddha, except he didn't use the name "Ganhwa Seon." The Buddha immersed himself in samadhi for six years pursuing one earnest question, "How can I become free from birth, ageing, sickness and death?" He was so completely focused on this question that he was not even aware that birds had built a nest in his hair. He then discarded all the practices he had cultivated up till then, and for seven days concentrated on the question that had propelled him forward on his spiritual quest his whole life: "How to become liberated from birth, ageing, sickness and death?" Then one morning, he suddenly saw the morning star shining in the eastern sky, attained great enlightenment and saw his true nature. This is exactly the Dharma of seeing one's true nature through Ganhwa Seon. After this pivotal moment, the Buddha demonstrated his mastery of the realm of supreme truth through three events, and transmitted this mastery through this Dharma of seeing one's true nature. The three cardinal events wherein the Buddha transmitted his mind directly were: when Mahakasyapa smiled while Buddha held up a lotus flower, when he shared the half of his seat with Mahakasyapa in front of the Pagoda of Many Children, and when Buddha extended his two feet out of his coffin.

Therefore, I want all of you to take advantage of this great Dharma assembly of Seon practice, to correctly understand the value of Ganhwa Seon, and to sincerely work on a *hwadu* under the correct guidance.

Then, how can you practice Seon correctly? If you have already received a *hwadu*, observe it. If not, investigate the *hwadu*,

"What is my true self before I was born of my parents?"

Investigate it with an earnest mind welling up from the depth of your heart, asleep or awake. The moment one cannot follow an inhalation with an exhalation, the physical body dies and the next life begins. Birth and death are like changing clothes. Because we keep alternating between them, neither is rightfully our true self. Thus, we must discover our eternal and immutable true self.

Therefore, in daily life we must ceaselessly remind ourselves to investigate the *hwadu*, "What is your true self before you are born of your parents?" We must do this a thousand times or even ten thousand times, and sustain and magnify the doubt that arises from our questioning. Let us take the example of a mill in a rural village to help explain this.

Suppose you want to grind some grain. Once the motor that turns the millstone is turned on, it can run all day with no problem. Likewise, in your unceasing effort to investigate a *hwadu*, there comes a moment when true questioning or true doubt is set in motion. In this way, when single-minded focus on a *hwadu* is turned on, then, like the running waters of a stream, doubt about one's *hwadu* flows without disruption.

At this time, even if objects are visible, you don't have the sense of seeing them, even if sounds are audible, you don't have the sense of hearing them. You become deaf, dumb and blind, like a log or a rock; you become unable to see or hear but have only a single-minded doubt about your *hwadu*. In this state a year may pass, and then ten years. Then suddenly, the opportune moment comes to see an object or hear a sound, and your *hwadu* is shattered; you penetrate through it to the home of the mind. Without having moved an inch, you are in the realm of the Buddhas and are in the same league as all Buddhas and Patriarchs. This is "seeing one's true nature."

All Buddhas and Patriarchs taught and transmitted this profound and sublime Dharma of seeing one's true nature, and this Dharma only exists now in Korea. As such, you must realize how fortunate you are to have encountered this precious Dharma, and you must not be distracted by other minor practices that utilize mindfulness. Because you are born as a human, which rarely happens in consecutive lifetimes, you must consider this life a forfeit and dedicate it wholly to practice, as if you didn't have this life, and resolve here and now to attain the great path of the Buddha and persevere accordingly.

To give you a good example of the correct practice of Ganhwa Seon, I'd like to tell you how this mountain monk sought the Path. I was born and grew up in Namhae, an island village off the southern coast of Gyeongsangnam-do Province. One day, I went with a relative to a small hermitage called Haegwan-am, about two miles from my house, where he often went to attend Buddhist services. There I met Seon Master Seogu Bohwa (石友 普化; 1875~1958), who later became my teacher.

At that time, Seon Master Seogu was greatly revered by both lay and ordained Buddhists and was renowned as a great sage. As such, whenever a three-month retreat ended, many Seon practitioners came to see him to have him assess their level of development, regardless of the long distance to Namhae.

When Master Seogu saw me, he immediately said, "Secular life is good, but there is even a worthier life. Would you like to give it a try?"

I asked, "What is this life you regard much worthier?"

He said, "There is a way that makes an ordinary person a great Buddha. Why don't you pretend that you have not been born at all in this life and devote it wholly to seeking this marvelous way?"

I was captivated by these words of the Seon Master, though I didn't know exactly why. I carefully observed how monks lived and found out that they lived a life of purity befitting Buddhist practitioners, rare in the secular world. Then, a great joy arose from within, and I made up my mind. I received permission from my parents to begin monastic life as a postulant. Every day I busied myself with serving the Seon Master, working as a cook, securing firewood and growing vegetables.

When Seon Master Seogu was invited to be the most senior teacher of Haein-sa Monastery in 1954, I followed him there to serve him and received the novice precepts that same year.

Later, Seon Master Seogu was appointed the first Supreme Patriarch of the Jogye Order and moved to Donghwa-sa Monastery. I continued to serve as his attendant and cook. One day, when some monks went hiking on Mt. Palgongsan on New year's Eve, I joined them without telling my master. On our way down the mountain, we stopped by a mountain hut where a monk used to practice. The hut was vacant, but some food had been left behind. A few monks proposed that we practice intense *hwadu* investigation there without sleeping for a week, and the whole group agreed. So I was away for a week without letting my master know my whereabouts and without his permission. Master Seogu was furious and admonished me saying, "You don't listen to your elders and want to do things your own way." Still, he recognized my will to practice Seon and gave me the *hwadu*, "What is your true self before you are born of your parents?"

Later, when I was 24 years old (1957), I finished all my courses at the Lecture Hall (now called "monastic college") and then finished a three month summer retreat. With the permission of the Supreme Patriarch, I embarked on a Seon journey and wandered like rain and clouds. At first, I went to Dongam Hermitage at Gakhwa-sa Temple, both of which were vacant at the time. Upon arriving at Dongam, I found a pile of small potatoes covered with a straw bag. I decided to cast off all involvement with the outside world and persevere in my Seon practice alone while sustaining myself on the potatoes. I practiced day and night for a couple of months in this fashion. Then one day, a spiritual friend, who had become the abbot of Gakhwa-sa, came to Dongam to see me. Worried about my lack of food, he visited me several times and suggested I go down to the main temple and live with him. Sensing that I could not maintain my practice with these visits, I moved to Dori-sa Temple in Seonsan.

At Dori-sa, I began a three month winter retreat with seven to eight other practitioners. When the scheduled sessions ended at 9 p.m., I went to bed with the others and lay down for a while. Then, when all the others were asleep, I arose quietly and practiced walking outside for a few hours. In this way I worked on my *hwadu* meticulously every day. Then one day, I had a small spark of insight during practice, and from this, I deluded myself into thinking, "I have seen it." I stopped observing the *hwadu* altogether and just waited for the end of the retreat. Meanwhile, I received a notice that Master Seogu, my teacher and first Supreme Patriarch of the Jogye Order, had passed away. So I went back to Donghwa-sa and participated in his Buddhist funeral ceremony.

Afterward, I visited Master Hyanggok Hyerim (香谷蕙林; 1912~1978), who was renowned as a great sage at that time. He was presiding at Myogwaneum-sa in Wollae, Gyeongsangnam-do Province. Upon seeing me, Seon Master Hyanggok said abruptly, "I will give you 30 blows if you speak correctly, and I will still give you 30 blows if you don't speak correctly. What will you do?" I didn't know what to say and hesitated. Then, Master Hyanggok asked me again by quoting a public case ("*gongan*") wherein Master Nanquan cut a cat in two.

That story goes like this: A long time ago in China, 700 monks practiced Seon under the tutelage of Seon Master Nanquan. There was a cat in the temple. Disputes often broke out over this cat as the monks of the Eastern Hall claimed the cat was theirs, and the monks of the Western Hall also claimed the cat. One day, Master Nanquan witnessed this dispute and instructed his attendant to ring the bell to gather all the monks. Seven hundreds monks stopped what they were doing and gathered at the Dharma Hall. Master Nanquan ascended the Dharma seat and said to his attendant, "Go get the cat and bring a knife." When the attendant produced the cat and the knife to Master Nanquan, he held the cat up and said:

"The monks practicing in the Eastern Hall claim that this cat is theirs while the monks practicing in the Western Hall also claim it as theirs. If you can speak correctly about this cat, I won't cut it. But if you can't, I will slash it in two."

Although 700 monks had argued over the ownership the cat, no one knew what Master Nanquan meant by holding up the cat and urging them to speak. When no reply came, Master

Nanquan held the cat up and cut it in two with his knife as he had promised and tossed it away. After he had returned to his room and rested, his favored disciple, Zhaozhou, who had not witnessed the incident due to other business, came to see him. After Zhaozhou paid his respects, Master Nanquan spoke of the incident, saying, "Today I gave a Dharma talk on the cat. If you had been there, what would you have said when I held up the cat and urged them to speak?" Zhaozhou immediately took off his sandals, put them on his head, and left the room. Master Nanquan said, "If you had been with the assembly at that time, you could have saved the cat."

Seon Master Hyanggok asked this mountain monk, "Speak about Seon Master Zhaozhou's response where he put his sandals on his head and left the room when asked to give an answer about Master Nanquan's holding up the cat." Again, I was not able to give a correct answer. I was still full of confidence that "I had seen it," but I was at a loss of how to answer. Nevertheless, as I was still lacking faith in virtuous teachers, I was unable to let go of this idea that I had seen it. Afterward, I wandered to many Seon monasteries and visited many eminent monks who were renowned as virtuous teachers.

육환장을 든 종정 예하

Master Jinje holding the six-ringed staff

In this wandering, I wasted more than two years.

I turned 26 and spent a three-month winter retreat at Sangwon-sa Monastery on Mt. Odaesan with seven to eight Seon practitioners. Accommodations were so scarce that we slept covering only our abdomens with the single cushion we used during meditation practice in the dead of a bitterly cold winter. We managed three months with just our daily rice and one side dish of cabbage kimchi. The only exception was when we made tofu as a communal activity. Fruit was also so rare that for three months each of us had only one and a half apples, that the proctor monk brought back from a trip. It was so cold that the drinking water left in our room often froze, and when it snowed, snow piled up to the eaves. We studied under harsh conditions that are unimaginable to contemporary society.

In the midst of our deprivation, there was one extraordinarily warm day. I sat on the wooden veranda that faces south and reflected upon my practice. I wondered, "Have I really seen my true nature? If I have, I should be able to give correct answers lightning-quick to all *gongans*. Why can't I? I must not deceive myself. To do so is wrong. If I am satisfied with this kind of attainment, I am useless. I must begin anew. If I deceive myself as well as others, I am guilty of a grave sin." In this way, I came to repent of my foolishness.

After I decided to let go of the illusion that "I had seen it," I began my study anew. I clearly realized then that what I needed most was the guidance of a virtuous teacher in order not to delude myself as I had before. Then, I began to have firm faith in Master Hyanggok who was the only teacher who responded swiftly with "right" or "wrong" to my replies in our previous question and answer sessions. So, upon the end of the winter retreat, I visited Master Hyanggok.

After paying my respects, I said, "I came to study with you and to rely on your guidance until I finish this great work. Please give me a *hwadu*."

Master Hyanggok answered, "How can you penetrate this difficult barrier of a *gongan*? You can't." Again I reaffirmed my resolve, saying, "I will work on it with my whole being. Until I penetrate this *gongan*, I won't leave the mountain gate with my sack." Then, Master Hyanggok gave me the *hwadu*, "Xiangyan Goes Up a Tree."

That story goes like this:

Someone is up in a very tall tree, hanging from a branch by

his mouth. He doesn't grasp the limb with his hands; his feet don't rest on a branch. At that time, someone under the tree asks him, "Why did Bodhidharma come from the West?" If he doesn't answer, he goes against the intention of the questioner, but if he does answer to the question, then he will fall to the ground from a great height of cliff and lose his life. What would you do in such a situation?"

I studied this *hwadu* for over two years as though my life depended on it. Then one autumn day when I was 28 years old, I was on my way to attend the early morning Dharma service when I tripped over a rock. As I picked myself up, the *hwadu* was finally shattered. All the wrong answers I had previously given were now resolved. It was at that moment that I discovered the "taste of Seon" that practitioners often referred to. What I had known before was nothing compared to my new understanding. So I composed a poem and offered it to Master Hyanggok:

How many people have known the truth of this Dharma staff?
None of the Buddhas of past, present or future do.
Suddenly this Dharma staff transforms into a golden dragon,

Performing innumerable wonders of the dragon entirely at will.

When Seon Master Hyanggok read it, he didn't ask any questions about the first half of the verse, but inquired about the last two lines, "What would you do if a Garuda, which swallows dragons, suddenly appeared before you?"

I answered, "Being cowered and disconcerted, I would withdraw three steps."

To this, Master Hyanggok was overjoyed saying, "That is so right!"

After breaking through my *hwadu*, I was having a Seon dialogue with Seon Master Hyanggok one day and was stymied again by the following story:

Seon Master Mazu, a great master of Tang China, fell ill right before he passed away. The proctor monk paid his respects in the morning and asked, "How is the venerable this morning?"

Master Mazu replied, "Sun-faced Buddha, Moon-faced Buddha."

Why did Master Mazu reply with the names of two Buddhas?

This *hwadu* encompasses highly advanced Dharma teaching that is most difficult to penetrate. Master Mazu had 84 outstanding students and was highly regarded by generations of enlightened teachers as the most exceptional sage of his time, after the Buddha. In this Dharma teaching about the Sun-faced Buddha and Moon-faced Buddha is contained the whole breadth of his attainment and practice. That is why it is often said that one must understand this dialogue if one wants to understand Master Mazu properly.

This mountain monk was also stymied by this dialogue and struggled with it for about five years. I questioned this *hwadu* day and night. In the old days, hardly any snow fell at Myogwaneum-sa Temple. One day in the first lunar month, I rose and opened the door and came out of the room in the early morning to find the whole mountains heavily covered with snow. However, in the big water-filled pot in the courtyard, there was no trace of snow as it had all melted upon hitting the water. The moment I saw the water, the *hwadu* was shattered. At long last, all possible variations of the Dharma talk by the ancient sages were penetrated in my mind. So I composed a verse and offered it to Master Hyanggok:

One strike of this Seon staff, the peak of Mt. Biro collapses,
One thunderous roar crushes ten million Dharma teachings.
In this small thatched hut, I lie down stretching my legs.
A cool breeze over the ocean remains fresh for ten thousand years.

Upon reading the verse, Master Hyanggok said, "This verse completely contains the legacy of the Sixth Patriarch, Mazu and Linji to whom was transmitted the Buddha's Dharma of the mind. He further praised me, saying, "The legacy of Seon will spread far and wide during your generation."

At the end of the 1967 three-month summer retreat, Seon Master Hyanggok ascended to the Dharma seat to give a talk. I went forward, offered three prostrations and asked:

"I'd like to ask a question to the honorable Seon Master. I don't want to ask about what all the Buddhas and the Patriarchs knew. However, I humbly ask you to speak a word of profound truth that all the Buddhas and the Patriarchs did not know."

"Nine times nine equals eighty-one," he said.

"That is a truth the Buddhas and Patriarchs already knew," I said.

"Six times six equals thirty-six," he said.

Without a word, I bowed and withdrew. Without a word, he descended from the Dharma seat and returned to his room.

The next day, I visited Seon Master Hyanggok in his room and with appropriate respect asked, "I'm not going to ask about the Buddha eye and the wisdom eye. However, what is the eye of this patched-robe monk?"

"The role of bhikkhunis is supposed to be performed by women," he said.

"Today I saw you in person for the first time," I said.

"Where did you see me?" he asked.

I shouted, "Kwan (關)!" (The bolt that locks the gate)

Saying, "That's right, that's right!" Master Hyanggok then entrusted me with the Dharma lamp of the Linji lineage, gave me the new Dharma name Jinje, and bestowed on me a Dharma Transmission Verse. It was 1967 and I was 33 years old. [The 79th Dharma descendant of the Buddha]

> Entrustment to my Dharma Successor, Jinje Beobwon
> The great living truth of the Buddhas and patriarchs,
> Can be neither given nor taken.

> Now I entrust this living phrase of Dharma to you,
>
> Whether you furl or unfurl the exhibit of truth is entirely up to you.

After this mountain monk attained the Great Path, I realized that awakening to the supreme truth of the Buddha was impossible without the practice of Ganhwa Seon. There are various practices in Buddhism such as prayer, recitation of the names of the Buddhas and bodhisattvas, mantra recitation and Vipassana meditation. However, all of these practices must be cultivated unceasingly, life after life, because they are practices of expedient means based on the different capacities of practitioners.

You must understand that these practices are not the supreme practice that the Buddha transmitted to Mahakasyapa. There must be a reason why generations of patriarchs taught only Seon. The basic tenets and legacy of the Jogye Order are also in keeping with this supreme practice. Ganhwa Seon practice as performed by the Buddha is the shortcut that leads practitioners to the realm of the Buddha without having to move even one inch. The Dharma lineage of the Buddhas and Patriarchs is passed on through this practice.

Then again, Seon practice is never the exclusive domain of

monastics. It can be and must be practiced by anyone who can differentiate that honey is sweet and salt is salty.

The world has entered a new culture-oriented era. Western intellectuals and religious leaders have already begun to apply mind-cultivating practices in daily life, beyond religion, to attain peace of mind and wisdom. They now regard mental cultivation as the most important virtue of life. They also say that genuine world peace and mankind's future happiness can not be brought about by any one country, religion or power. Only mental cultivation and the spiritual growth of each individual will provide the correct solutions. Furthermore, the world is beginning to view Ganhwa Seon as a spiritual culture that can pioneer a brighter future for humanity, transcending religions and national boundaries.

Therefore, members of the assembly! All of you must cultivate your minds with Seon practice without regard to religious boundaries; you must awaken to the truth and achieve inner tranquility. If, up to now, we have concentrated on helping the marginalized and those in suffering, now is the time to take the practice of Seon practice to the world with all possible haste. Then we can contribute to genuine world peace and happiness.

My hope is for all people to grow in wisdom so that the Buddha Land and the Pure Land of Ultimate Bliss can be realized on this planet.

Seven days before he passed away, Master Hyanggok, the teacher of this mountain monk, went around to many Seon monasteries and tested their guiding teachers about the "Alms Round Conversation" from the Dharma talks of Seon Master Linji.

That story goes like this:

One day Master Linji went out asking for alms and knocked on the gate of a house. An old grandma opened the gate and abruptly shouted, "You are a shameless monk!" and did not give him even one coin.

Master Linji said, "How can you say I am shameless when you offer no alms?"

Without a word, the old woman slammed the gate on him and went inside. Master Linji returned in silence.

Master Hyanggok visited different guiding teachers all over the country and asked about this Dharma talk, but not a single answer was good enough for him. Lastly, he visited this mountain monk at Haeunjeong-sa Monastery in Busan. I was walking in the yard when he arrived. The moment he saw this mountain monk, he asked the same question. "If you had been Master Linji, what would you have said when the old woman slammed the gate on him and went inside?" Even before being seated and receiving my prostrations, he asked me this question while standing in the yard. This mountain monk could guess that he had not been satisfied with the responses of the other teachers, so I answered him before he even finished his question. Then he roared with laughter and said, "Indeed, you are my disciple!"

Monks of this assembly! What would you have said if you had been Seon Master Linji?

> **For thirty years I enjoyed riding a horse,**
> **Today I was greatly gored by a donkey.**

Once upon a time, two renowned teachers saw an eight-year-old girl who could not speak and offered their opinions about her silence. One said that the girl's inability to speak meant she had attained the truth of the Great Path. The other said she could not speak because it was difficult for her to attain the truth of the Great Path.

Assembly of monks! Which do you think is the better answer? Which answer do you think is right?

[Addressing the silent assembly,]

The winter solstice and the Day of Cold Food are 105 days apart.

All monks in presence! This mountain monk earnestly wishes that you seek your true self by investigating the *hwadu*, "What is my true self before I was born of my parents?" Investigate it for 1,000 or even 10,000 times every day. I pray that you attain great wisdom, life after life, and enjoy unlimited happiness.

[The Master hits the Dharma staff once and descends the Dharma Seat.]

뉴욕 리버사이드 교회에서 대중들에게 주장자를 들어 보이시는 모습, 2011

Master Jinje raises and shows the Dharma staff to the congregation:
Dharma assembly held at Riverside Church (New York, 2011)

세계 평화를 위한
간화선 대법회 상당법어

2011. 9. 15. 뉴욕, 리버사이드 교회

〔상당하시어 주장자를 들어 대중에게 보이시고〕

마음,

마음,

마음이여!

가히 찾기가 어려움이로다.

찾으려 한 즉슨 그대가 가히 보지 못함이로다.

무심히 앉아 있으니 마음도 무심히 앉아 있음이로다.

〔주장자를 바로 들어 보이시면서〕

대중은 보고, 보십시오.

이곳 리버사이드 교회에 가득 자리하신 선남선녀 여러분, 대단히 반갑습니다!

지금 여기에는 여러 종교인이 계시는 줄 알고 있습니다. 제가 이 자리에 선 이유는 어떤 종교가 더 낫고 낫지 않고를 가리려는 것이 아닙니다. 다만 세계 평화를 위해 동양의 정신문화를 소개해서 온 인류에게 공헌(貢獻)하고자 함입니다.

이제 세계는 종교와 사상을 넘어서 서로가 마음을 통하는 시대가 되었습니다. 그러므로 모든 종교는 인간 내면세계의 정화(淨化)와 좀 더 나은 세상을 만드는 일에 협력하는 우애로운 형제가 되고, 선한 이웃이 되어야 합니다.

금일 산승이 여러분께 소개하고자 하는 동양정신문화의 골수인 간화선은 모든 종교와 사상을 초월하여 참나를 깨달아 세계 평화를 이룰 수 있는 훌륭한 수행법입니다.

인인개개(人人箇箇)가 스스로 참나를 깨달아 마음의 고향에 이르면, 어머니의 품과 같이 온갖 시비 갈등과 시기와 질투가 끊어 없어져서 대안락과 대자유, 그리고 무량한 대지혜를 수용하게 됩니다.

참나를 깨닫는다고 하는 것은 지금 이 자리에서 산승의 법문을 듣고 있는 여러분이 삶의 주인공임을 깨닫는 것입니다. 그 주인공은 모든 곳에서 주인공이 되어, 삶의 많은 부분을 무애자재(無碍自在)하게 수용할 수 있게 됩니다. 그래서 어디에도 의존하지 않고,

모든 가치관에서 자유로운 사람이 되며, 모든 종교와 정치제도, 문화적 제약에서 벗어난 절대 자유인이 되는 것이니, 인류의 희망이 참나를 깨닫는 데 있고, 미래가 여기에서 열리게 되는 것입니다.

그러면 어떻게 해야 참나를 깨달아 마음의 고향에 이르러 다 같이 영원토록 평화를 누릴 수 있겠습니까?

참나를 깨달은 눈 밝은 '참스승'을 만나는 것이 가장 중요합니다. 광대무변(廣大無邊)하고 심오한 마음의 고향에 도달하는 것은 혼자의 힘으로서는 불가능하기 때문입니다.

이렇게 눈 밝은 스승을 만나 대오견성(大悟見性)의 발원(發願)을 확고히 하여 모든 분이 각자 일상생활 속에, '부모에게 나기 전에 어떤 것이 참나인가?' 하고 오매불망 간절히 의심해야 합니다. 이것을 일러 참선(參禪)이라고 합니다. 참선으로 일념이 지속되는 과정을 이루어야 마음의 고향에 이르게 되어 일월(日月)과 같은 밝은 지혜가 열리는 동시에 큰 자비와 사랑을 갖추게 되는 것입니다. 그러면 온 인류가 나와 더불어 한몸이 되고, 온 세계, 유정무정(有情無情)이 다 나와 더불어 한 집이 되어 대 평화를 성취하게 될 것입니다.

또한 옛 성인들이 말씀하시기를 "사람들이 빈한(貧寒)하게 사는 것은 지혜가 짧기 때문이다" 하셨으니, 모든 인류가 나고 날 적마다 출세와 복락을 누리고자 한다면 이처럼 마음의 고향에 이르는 밝은 지혜의 눈을 얻어야 할 것입니다.

그러면 참나를 깨닫기 위해서는 어떻게 닦아야 하는가?
우선 참선은 앉아서 익히기가 가장 쉽기 때문에 먼저 좌선을 익히도록 합니다. 아침저녁으로 좌복(坐服) 위에 반가부좌를 하고 앉아 허리를 곧게 하고 가슴을 편 다음 두 손은 모아서 단전 밑에 붙입니다.

눈은 2미터 아래에다 화두생각을 두고 응시하되, 혼침(昏沈)과 망상(妄想)에 떨어지지 않도록 눈을 뜨고 의심에 몰두해야 합니다.

이렇게 앉아서 무르익어지고 나면, 일상생활 속에서 가나오나, 앉으나 서나, 일을 하나, 산책을 하나, 잠을 자나, 오매불망 간절히 화두의심에 몰두해야 합니다.

이렇게 하루에도 천 번 만 번 '부모에게 나기 전에 어떤 것이 참나인가?'하고 의심을 쭉 밀고, 밀고, 또 밀 것 같으면 모든 산란심이 일어날 틈이 없게 됩니다. 비유하자면 시골의 방아 찧는 기계가 시동이 안 걸리면 방아를 찧지 못하지만, 한 번 시동이 걸리면 종일 방아를 찧을 수가 있는 것과 마찬가지입니다.

하루에도 천 번 만 번 의심을 밀어주라는 이유는, 그렇게 천 번 만 번 의심하여 단련이 되면 문득 참의심이 시동 걸리게 되어 화두의심 한 생각이 끊이지 않고 지속되는 과정이 오기 때문입니다. 마치 흐르는 시냇물과 같이 밤낮으로 한 생각이 흐르고 흐르게 되어 앉아 있어도 밤이 지나가는지 낮이 지나가는지 모르게 되고, 보고 듣는 모든 것을 다 잊어버리게 됩니다. 화두일념에 푹 빠져서 시간이 흐르고 흐르다가 홀연히 사물을 보는 찰나, 혹은 소리를 듣는 찰나에 화두가 박살이 나게 됩니다.

그렇게 되면 자연히 밝은 지혜의 눈이 열리어 억만년이 다하도록 항상 밝아 있게 되므로 만인에게 진리의 지도자, 하늘세계와 인간세계의 사표(師表)가 되어 자유자재로 활개를 치게 됩니다. 한 걸음도 옮기지 않고 마음의 고향에 이르면 자유와 행복과 세계 평화를 영원토록 누리게 되는 것입니다.

대중 여러분!

참나 속에 변치 않는 정의(正義)가 있으며, 참나 속에 영원한 행복이 있으며, 참나 속에 걸림 없는 대자유가, 참나 속에 밝은 지혜가, 참나 속에 모두가 평등한 참된 평화가 있습니다.

이러한 정의와 자유와 지혜와 평등과 행복은 아무리 학식이 풍부하고, 아무리 부유하고, 아무리 지위와 명성이 높고 성스럽게 산다 할지라도 누릴 수 있는 것이 아닙니다. 오직 참나를 깨달은 자만이 누릴 수 있습니다.

비록 이번 생에 화두일념삼매가 지속되는 과정을 이루지 못한다 할지라도, 온 인류가 생활 속에 꾸준히 참선수행을 닦아 행한다면 마음에 있는 모든 분별과 시비 갈등이 사라지게 되어 자연히 마음이 안정될 것입니다. 그러면 죽음에 다다라서도 밝은 마음, 맑은 정신으로 몸뚱이를 옷 갈아입듯 벗게 되고, 다음 생에는 반드시 진리를 깨닫게 될 것입니다. 그러나 이러한 참선수행을 등한시한다면 온갖 분별과 시비와 갈등에 하루뿐만이 아니라 일생을 헛되게 보내게 될 것이니, 그 결과는 고통과 갈등뿐이라서 죽음에 다다라 후회한들 이미 늦습니다.

따라서 모든 분이 간화선(看話禪)이라는 훌륭한 수행법을 꾸준히 닦아서 아이가 울면 자장가를 불러주는 가운데 화두를 챙기시고, 남편이 꾸짖을 적에도 화두를 챙기시고, 부인이 시비를 걸 때는 처사가 화두를 챙기시면 화목한 집안이 될 것입니다. 나아가 화목한 사회와 나라를 이루며 마침내 세계 평화에 큰 원동력이 될 것입니다.

대중 여러분!
여러분께 간화선 수행법에 대해 믿음과 확신을 드리고자 산승이 참선수행에 입문하고 수행하여 깨달은 기연(機緣)을 소개해 드릴까 합니다.

산승이 스무 살이 되던 정월 초에 친척 어른과 함께 남해 해관암을 찾아가 석우(石友) 선사를 친견하게 되었는데, 선사께서 산승을 보고 말씀하셨습니다.

"이보게 청년, 세상에 사는 것도 좋지만, 이번 생은 태어나지 않은 셈 치고 중노릇을 해 보지 않겠는가?"

그래서 제가 여쭈었습니다.

"중노릇하면 어떠한 좋은 점들이 있습니까?"

스님께서는 다음과 같이 말씀하셨습니다.

"범부가 위대한 부처 되는 법이 있네."

'범부가 위대한 부처가 된다'는 이 말에 왠지 마음이 끌렸습니다.

"부모님이 계시니, 가서 허락을 받아보도록 하겠습니다."

석우 선사께 이같이 말씀드리고는 스님들의 생활을 두루 살펴보았습니다. 세상 사람과 똑같이 밥을 먹고 살지만 판이한 생활을 하고 있었습니다. 스님들이 손수 빨래하고, 밥 짓고, 나무하고, 그 가운데 참선수행을 하고 있는데 그것은 세상 밖의 생활이었습니다. 전생의 인연인지 산승의 눈에는 수도하는 청정한 삶이 아주 아름답게 비쳤고, '범부가 위대한 부처된다'는 선사님의 말씀이 마음에 깊이 와 닿았습니다. 그래서 그 길로 집으로 돌아와 부모님께 허락을 얻은 후 출가하게 되었습니다.

그 후 "부모에게 나기 전에 어떤 것이 참나인가?"라는 화두를 받아 열심히 정진하던 중 견처(見處)가 생겨, 당시에 선지식으로는 이름이 가장 높았던 묘관음사의 향곡(香谷) 선사를 찾아갔습니다.

향곡 선사께서 대뜸 물으셨습니다.

"바른 답을 해도 삼십 방을 맞고, 바른 답을 못해도 삼십 방을 맞을 것이니, 어떻게 하겠느냐?"

산승이 말을 못하고 우물쭈물하였는데 다시 몇 가지를 물으셨습니다. 그래도 답을 못하니 향곡 선사께서 말씀하셨습니다.

"아니다. 공부를 다시 해라."

그래서 2년여 동안 제방(諸方)을 다니면서 수행하다가 다시금 큰 분심(憤心)을 내어 향곡 선사를 찾아갔습니다.

"화두를 하나 내려주십시오. 화두를 타파하기 전에는 바랑을 지지 않겠습니다."

아무리 팔풍(八風, 이익·손해·비방·찬탄·꾸지람·칭찬·괴로움·즐거움)이 불어 닥친다 해도 동요하지 않는다는 말이니, 이것은 아무나 할 수 있는 약조가 아닙니다. 그러니 향곡 선사께서 말씀하셨습니다.

"이 어려운 진리의 관문을 네가 어찌 해결할 수 있겠느냐?"

"생명을 떼 놓고 해보겠습니다. 화두를 하나 내려주십시오."

이렇게 간청 드리니, 산승의 참학의지(參學意志)를 간파하시고 '향엄상수화(香嚴上樹話)'라는 화두를 내려 주셨습니다. 이는 중국 당나라 때 위산 도인의 제자인 향엄(香嚴) 선사의 법문입니다.

어떤 스님이 아주 높은 나무에 올라가서, 손으로 나뭇가지를 잡지도 않고 발로 밟지도 않고 오직 입으로만 나뭇가지를 물고 매달려 있는데, 때마침 나무 밑을 지나가던 스님이 물었습니다.

"달마 스님이 서역에서 중국으로 오신 뜻이 무엇입니까?"

답을 하려니 수십 길 낭떠러지에 떨어져 몸이 박살이 날 것이고, 가만히 있으려니 묻는 이의 뜻에 어긋나고, 이러한 때를 당해서 어찌해야 하겠습니까?

이 화두를 받아서 2년 5개월 동안 결제 해제를 잊고, 산문을 나가지 않고 일구월심(日久月深) 화두와 씨름을 했습니다. 그러다 하루는 새벽에 일어나서 부처님 전에 예불하러 가는데, 도량(道場)이 어두워서 돌부리에 걸려 넘어졌다 일어나는 순간 홀연히 화두가 타파(打破)되었습니다. 그리하여 그 깨달은 경지를 글로 써서 향곡 선사께 올렸습니다.

이 주장자 이 진리를 몇 사람이나 알꼬?
과거, 현재, 미래의 모든 부처님도 다 알지 못함이로다.
한 막대기 주장자가 문득 금빛 용이 되어서
한량없는 용의 조화를 마음대로 부림이로다.

자개주장기인회(這箇拄杖幾人會)아
삼세제불총불식(三世諸佛總不識)이라.
일조주장화금룡(一條拄杖化金龍)이니
응화무변임자재(應化無邊任自在)로다.

한 몽둥이 휘둘러 비로정상을 거꾸러뜨리고
벽력 같은 일 할로써 천만 갈등을 문대버림이로다.
두 칸 띠암자에 다리 펴고 누웠으니
바다 위 맑은 바람 만년토록 새롭도다.

일봉타도비로정(一棒打倒毘盧頂)하고

일할말각천만측(一喝抹却千萬則)이라.
이간모암신각와(二間茅庵伸脚臥)하니
해상청풍만고신(海上淸風萬古新)이로다.

이렇게 적어서 향곡선사께 갖다 바치니 용(龍)의 조화(造化)를 들어서 물으셨습니다. 용의 조화는 산을 떠 오기도 하고 산을 없애기도 하고 비를 내리기도 하고 거두기도 하는 것입니다.

"너 문득 용 잡아먹는 금시조를 만나서는 어떻게 하려는고?"

산승이 즉시 대답했습니다.

"전신을 굽히고 움츠려 당황하여 몸을 세 걸음 물러갑니다(屈節當胸退身三步)."

하니, 이에 향곡선사께서 "옳고, 옳다. 모든 성인의 진리의 가풍이 이 게송(偈頌) 중에 다 있구나. 장차 너로 인해 참선법이 크게 흥하리라."

라고 하시며, 만 사람을 지도할 안목을 갖췄다는 법을 전하는 인증서를 내리셨습니다.

부처님과 도인의 산 진리는
전할 수도 없고 또한 받을 수도 없나니
이제 그대에게 산 진리를 전하노니
만인 앞에 진리의 전(廛)을 펴거나 거두거나 그대에게 맡기노라.

불조대활구(佛祖大活句)는
무전역무수(無傳亦無受)라.
금부활구시(今付活句時)에
수방임자재(收放任自在)로다.

이때가 산승의 나이 33세였습니다. 이렇게 참선공부를 해서 진리를 깨달아 먼저 깨달은 스승에게 인증을 받는 가풍이 석가여래로부터 2,500년이 넘는 세월 동안 전해 내려오는 전통입니다.

여러분들도 '부모에게 나기 전에 어떤 것이 참나인가?'라는 화두를 타파하여 점검을 받아 바른 눈을 갖춘다면, 만 사람의 눈을 멀지 않게 하고 진리의 바른 지도자가 될 수 있습니다.

뉴욕 리버사이드 교회에서 종정 예하의 법문을 듣고 있는 미국의 청중들, 2011
American Audience gathered at Riverside Church to hear Master Jinje's teaching

약 100여 년 전 한국에 만공(滿空) 선사라는 도인 스님이 계셨는데, 수십 명 대중에게 항시 바른 수행을 지도하고 계셨습니다. 하루는 몇몇 수좌들과 마루에 앉아 한담을 하는 중에 처마 끝에 새가 푸르륵 날아가니 만공 선사께서 물으셨습니다.

"저 새가 하루에 몇 리나 날아가는고?"

여러분 가운데도 답할 분이 있으면 한 번 답을 해 보십시오. 이 물음에 다른 수좌들은 답이 없었는데 보월(寶月) 선사가 일어나 다음과 같이 명답을 했습니다.

"촌보(寸步)도 처마를 여의지 아니했습니다."

훗날 만공 선사께서 열반에 드시니 산중회의를 해서 고봉(高峯) 선사를 진리의 지도자인 조실(祖室)로 모시기로 하였습니다. 결제일이 도래하여 대중이 고봉 선사께 법문을 청하니, 고봉 선사가 법문을 위해 일어나서 법상에 오르려 하였습니다. 바로 그때 금오(金烏) 선사가 뒤를 따라가서 고봉 선사의 장삼 자락을 잡으면서 말했습니다.

"선사님, 법상에 오르기 전에 한 말씀 이르고 오르십시오."

"장삼 자락 놔라!"

고봉 선사가 이렇게 말하니, 금오 선사가 재차 물었습니다.

"한 말씀 이르고 오르십시오."

"장삼 자락 놔라!"

그 후로 40년 세월이 흘러 하루는 산승의 스승이신 향곡 선사께서 산승에게 이 대문을 들어서 물으셨습니다.

"네가 만약 당시에 고봉 선사였다면 금오 선사가 장삼 자락을 붙잡고 한마디 이르고 오르라 할 때에 뭐라고 하려는고?"

향곡 선사의 물음이 떨어지자마자 산승은 벽력같이 '할(喝)'을 했습니다.

"억!" 하고 할을 하니, 향곡 선사께서 말씀하셨습니다.

"네가 만약 그렇게 할을 한다면 세상 사람의 눈을 다 멀게 하여 가리라."

할이 틀렸다는 말입니다. 향곡 선사의 이 같은 말씀에 산승이 바로 말씀드렸습니다.

"소승(小僧)의 허물입니다."

그러자 향곡 선사께서 멋지게 회향하셨습니다.

"노승(老僧)의 허물이니라."

자고로 법담(法談)은 이렇게 나가야 합니다.

장삼 자락을 붙잡고 '이르라' 할 때에는 한마디 척 해야 하는데, 산승이 즉시 '할'을 한 것은 묻는 상대의 안목을 한 번 흔들어 놓는 것입니다. 즉 묻는 사람이 알고 묻느냐 알지 못하고 묻느냐, 알아보기 위한 것입니다.

그러자 향곡 선사께서는 바로 낙처(落處)를 아시고는 '네가 만약 그렇게 후학을 지도한다면 앞으로 만 사람의 눈을 멀게 하여간다'고 바르게 점검하신 것입니다. 눈 밝은 이는 이렇게 흑백을 척척 가릴 수 있어야 선지식이 되고 만 사람의 바른 지도자가 될 수가 있는 것입니다. 그러나 그러한 눈이 없다면 태산(太山)이 가리고 있어서 선지식 노릇을 할 수 없는 법입니다.

향곡 선사의 말씀에 산승이 '소승의 허물입니다' 하고 바로 잘못을 거두니, 향곡 선사께서도 '노승의 허물이니라' 하고 바로 거두셨으니, 이 얼마나 멋지게 주고받은 진리의 문답입니까!
여러분, 이 대문을 바로 보십시오!

한때 전국의 발심한 스님네 삼사십 명이 한국의 양주 망월사에 모여 대오견성(大悟見性)을 위해 산문 출입을 금한 뒤 생사를 떼어 놓고 용맹정진에 들어가게 되었습니다. 용성(龍城) 선사를 조실로, 훗날 조계종 초대종정이신 석우(石友) 선사를 선덕으로, 운봉(雲峰) 선사를 입승으로 모시고 여법히 참선정진에 임한 지 반살림이 도래하게 되었습니다. 반살림 법회날 조실 스님께서 법상에 오르셔서 법문하시며 다음과 같은 물음을 던지셨습니다.
"나의 참모습은 삼세의 모든 성인도 보지 못함이요, 역대의 도인들도 보지 못하나니, 여기 모인 모든 대중은 어느 곳에서 산승의 참모습을 보려는고?"
이에 운봉 선사가 일어나서 명답을 하였습니다.
"유리독 속에 몸을 감췄습니다."
그러자 용성 조실 스님께서는 아무런 점검도 하시지 않고 즉시 법상에서 내려와 조실방으로 돌아가 버리셨습니다.

그러한 법석이 있고 40년 세월이 흐른 후에 향곡 선사께서 산승에게 물으셨습니다.

"네가 만약 그 당시에 용성 선사였다면, '유리독 속에 몸을 감췄다'고 하신 답에 대해 뭐라고 점검하고 내려가겠느냐?"

향곡 선사께서 보는 눈이 있어서 이렇게 물으신 것입니다.

용성 선사께서 아무런 말없이 내려간 그것도 물론 잘한 것이지만, 향곡 선사께서는 달리 보시는 바가 있어 산승에게 물으신 것입니다. 그래서 산승이 답하였습니다.

"'눈 밝은 도인이 아주 멋진 답을 하였습니다' 이렇게 점검을 하고 내려가겠습니다."

이에 향곡 선사께서 크게 칭찬하셨습니다.

대중 여러분!
"나의 참모습은 모든 성인도 보지 못하고 모든 도인도 보지 못하나니 어느 곳에서 나의 참모습을 보려는고?" 하고 물어올 때,

여러분이라면 무엇이라고 답을 하시겠습니까? 답할 자가 있으면 답을 해 보십시오.

대중 가운데 한 사람이 일어나서 "큰스님!"하고 부르니

진제 대선사께서 "불시(不是)라, 산승을 부름은 옳지 못하도다."

그 사람이 "아이고, 아이고!" 하고 곡을 하니,

진제 대선사께서 "가까이 있으면 이 주장자로 삼십 방을 맞아야

옳도다!"

[한참을 계시다가 이르시기를]

그러면 산승이 대신해서 한마디 하겠습니다.

"시자야! 빗장을 잘 잠가라."

아시겠습니까?

몇 해 전 이곳 미국에서 9·11테러로 많은 분이 희생되었습니다. 돌아가신 고귀한 영혼들을 위해 고준(高峻)한 법문을 선사하도록 하겠습니다.

9·11테러로 인한 희생자 모든 영령이시여, 태어남과 죽음이 본래로 있는 것이 아니요, 사대(四大)도 본래 없는 것이고 오온(五蘊)도 있는 것이 아님이니, 모든 애착과 미움과 원한들을 다 놓고 산승의 고준한 법문을 잘 받아가시셔서 정토의 세계에서 영원토록 편안한 낙을 누리소서.

필경(畢竟)에 진리의 한 마디는 어떠한 것인고?

산봉우리에 구름이 걷히니 산마루가 드러나고
밝은 달은 물결 위에 떠 있음이로다.

무운생령상(無雲生嶺上)하고

유월낙파심(唯月落波心)이라

What is your true self?

(무엇이 참나인고?)

[잠시 후]

Thank you very much.

(대단히 감사합니다.)

[주장자로 법상을 한 번 치고 하좌하시다.]

뉴욕 리버사이드 교회에서 상당법문하시는 모습, 2011

Master Jinje giving a Dharma talk:
The Dharma Assembly held at Riverside Church (New York, 2011)

World Peace through Ganhwa Seon

September 15, 2011, at Riverside Church, New York City

Mind, Mind, Mind!

So difficult to find,

Try, but you'll never see it

Just sit in no-mind,

Mind sits right there too.

Ladies and gentlemen, look, look!

As I begin, I would first like to express my gratitude and delight to all of you, who have taken time out to be in attendance here tonight at Riverside Church. I am aware that many different religious leaders have come also. This mountain monk has come to this sacred site not to compare different religious traditions and talk about which one is superior, but to introduce you to the spiritual culture of Asia as one step in the process of fostering world peace.

Not limiting ourselves by ideology or religious doctrine, soon we will be able to communicate directly, mind to mind. All religions should act as siblings and good neighbors, helping each other to find inner peace, making the world a better place.

Tonight, this mountain monk would like to introduce "questioning meditation" or what we Koreans call Ganhwa Seon. This is the heart of our spiritual culture in Asia. Ganhwa Seon is a superb practice which transcends religion and ideology. It will create understanding and generate world peace as well as guide us to awakening. When you awaken to your true self and arrive at the mind's home, then, like a child in their mother's arms, all kinds of arguments disappear. There is no conflict, jealousy, or envy here; you will be able to enjoy peace and freedom while displaying great wisdom.

Awakening to true self means to awaken to the master within. I ask each of you, "What is sitting here listening to me speak right now?" When you awaken to this master within, it will become the master everywhere, living a free life without hindrance. By not relying on anything but this unchangeable true self, you will be liberated from all religious, political, and cultural restraints and live harmoniously with all beings. Awakening to the true self is the hope for the human race; from here, the future will open up.

So, how can we awaken to true self and arrive at the home of mind? How can we enjoy great peace forever?

The most important thing is to first meet an authentic, clear-eyed teacher who has awakened to true self. The mind's true home is so vast and boundless, profound and recondite, it is impossible to arrive there through one's own power alone. You must meet a clear-eyed teacher and firmly make a vow that you will attain great awakening and see your own true nature. Question the following topic, or *hwadu*, without ever forgetting it:

"What is your true self before you are born of your parents?"

This inquiry is what we call Ganhwa Seon. By constantly maintaining single-minded concentration through Ganhwa Seon, you will arrive at the mind's home; wisdom shining like the sun and the moon will radiate from you while simultaneously attaining great compassion and love. In this state, you will become one body with the whole human race; one household with all sentient and insentient being. This is how we will be able to bring great peace to the world.

As an ancient sage said, "People live in poverty because of lack of wisdom." If people want to be successful, enjoy good fortune and receive blessings in their life, then they must arrive at the mind's home and attain the eye of marvelous wisdom.

How do we practice in order to awaken to true self?

The easiest way to practice Seon is by sitting meditation, so you must learn how to do this correctly. Sit comfortably on your mat in the morning and evening. Straighten your back, expand your chest, and place both hands on your lap below your navel. Look six feet in front of you and focus your concentration on your topic of inquiry, the *hwadu*, at that spot. Concentrate with your eyes open so that you don't succumb to drowsiness or distracting thoughts. While continuing to sit, extend your practice to fill every moment.

Whether you're coming or going, sitting or standing, working or sleeping, you earnestly focus on questioning your *hwadu* without ever forgetting it. In this way, keep pushing forward again and again, raising the question about the *hwadu*: "What is your true self before you are born of your parents?" Continue to bring it up tens of thousands of times without ever forgetting it;

there will be no space for any distraction to arise. To give you an example, it is like a mill stone in a grain mill; if the water wheel is not turning, the mill stone will not grind the grain, but once the wheel starts turning, the mill stone will grind grain all day long. In the same way, I tell you to keep pushing forward with the question tens of thousands of times because once you become trained in this kind of questioning, all of a sudden you will reach a new point in your practice: true questioning. The questioning of the *hwadu* will not cease for even a moment, but will flow continuously. This single-minded questioning will keep flowing along day and night just like a running stream. When you are sitting in Seon, you will be unaware whether it is day or night; you will forget everything you see and hear. In this way, you become completely absorbed in the single-minded questioning of *hwadu*. As time passes, there will ultimately be an instant when, upon seeing an object or hearing a sound, your *hwadu* will unexpectedly shatter.

At that point, the eye of wisdom naturally opens and will remain forever brilliant. You will then guide all people to the Truth. As a great teacher in both Heaven and Earth, you will be completely free and unhindered. In this way, when you reach the mind's home without taking a single step, you will enjoy glorious freedom and happiness. You will truly contribute to peace for all humankind.

In true self, there is immutable integrity. In true self, there is eternal happiness. In true self, there is great freedom that is devoid of all hindrances. In true self, there is true peace that comes from complete impartiality. Such integrity, happiness, freedom, and impartiality can not be obtained merely through education or wealth, how devoutly you live your life, or through your position or sterling reputation. Rather, only a person who has awakened to true self can be so blessed.

Even if in this lifetime you do not attain the state of single-minded samadhi on the *hwadu*, if you are to practice Ganhwa Seon continuously throughout your everyday lives, then all discrimination, disputes, and conflicts will disappear and your minds will naturally be in repose. At the moment of death, with a clear mind and bright spirit, you will let go of this physical body, just as if you are changing clothes; and in the next life you will definitely attain great awakening.

However, if you neglect Seon practice, you will waste your life in discriminations, disputes, and conflicts. The result will just be suffering and remorse. On your deathbed, it will be too late to have regrets about how you wasted your life.

Thus, I hope all of you will continuously cultivate this practice of Ganhwa Seon, questioning meditation, so that you will learn to hold the *hwadu* even when you are singing a lullaby to a crying baby, or maintaining your marriage. By living this way, you'll have a commendable family and your household will live in perfect concord. If everyone practices like this, then our society and country will also be in perfect harmony; this will become a driving force in forging world peace.

To give you a good example of the correct practice of Ganhwa Seon, I'd like to tell you how this mountain monk sought the Path.

When I was twenty, I went with a relative to a small hermitage called Haegwan-am one Lunar New Year's Day. When Master Seogu Bohwa (石友普化; 1875~1958) saw me, he immediately said, "Secular life is good, but would you like to consider this life a forfeit and dedicate it wholly to being a monk?"

I asked, "What is so good about being a monk?"

He said, "It is a way that makes an ordinary person a great Buddha."

I was captivated by these words of the Seon Master, though I didn't know exactly why, so I responded, "My parents are still alive, so I must ask their permission."

Then I carefully observed how monks lived. The monks were doing their own laundry and preparing meals, but during those everyday events, they were also doing Seon meditation practice; they lived a life of purity befitting Buddhist practitioners, rare in the secular world. Perhaps due to past karma, a great joy arose from within me, and what the Seon Master had told me about an ordinary person becoming a great Buddha resonated deeply within me. So, I received permission from my parents to begin monastic life as a postulant.

Once I became a monk, I received the *hwadu*, "What is your true self before you are born of your parents?" After a while, when I thought I had a certain measure of understanding, I visited Master Hyanggok Hyerim (香谷蕙林; 1912~1978), who was renowned as a great sage at that time. Upon seeing me, Seon Master Hyanggok said abruptly, "I will give you 30 blows if you speak correctly, and I will still give you 30 blows if you don't speak correctly. What will you do?" I didn't know what to say and hesitated. Seon Master Hyanggok then said, "You're not ready. Go and practice some more." So I practiced ardently for two more years and once again I sought out Seon Master Hyanggok. After paying my respects, I said, "I came to study with you and to rely on your guidance until I finish this great work. Please give me a *hwadu*."

Master Hyanggok answered, "How can you penetrate this difficult barrier of a *gongan*? You can't." Again I reaffirmed my resolve, saying, "I will work on it with my whole being. Until I penetrate this *gongan*, I won't exit the mountain gate with my sack. This meant, I would not be swayed by the eight worldly dharmas (praise and ridicule, pleasure and suffering, good reputation and defamation, gain and loss)."

Then, Master Hyanggok gave me the *hwadu*, "Xiangyan Goes Up a Tree."

That story goes like this:

A monk is up in a very tall tree, hanging from a branch by his mouth. He doesn't grasp the limb with his hands; his feet don't rest on a branch. At that time, another monk under the tree asks him, "What is the meaning of Bodhidharma coming from the west?" If he doesn't answer, he goes against the intention of the questioner, but if he does answer to the question, then he will fall to the ground from a great height and lose his life. What would you do in such a situation?"

I wrestled with this *hwadu* for over two years and five months as though my life depended on it. Then one autumn day when I was 28 years old, I was on my way to attend the early morning Dharma service when I tripped over a rock. As I picked myself up, the *hwadu* was finally shattered. All the wrong answers I had previously given were now resolved. It was at that moment that I discovered the "taste of Seon" that practitioners often referred to. What I had known before was nothing compared to my new understanding. So I composed a verse and offered it to Master Hyanggok:

How many people have known the truth of this Dharma staff?
None of the Buddhas of past, present or future do.
Suddenly this Dharma staff transforms into a golden dragon,
Performing innumerable wonders of the dragon entirely at will.

One strike of this Seon staff, the peak of Mt. Biro collapses,
One thunderous roar crushes ten million Dharma teachings.
In this small thatched hut, I lie down stretching my legs.
A cool breeze over the ocean remains fresh for ten thousand years.

When Seon Master Hyanggok read it, he inquired, "What would you do if a Garuda, which swallows dragons, suddenly appeared before you?"

I answered, "Being cowered and disconcerted, I would withdraw three steps."

To this, Master Hyanggok was overjoyed and said, "That is so right! This verse completely contains the legacy of the Sixth Patriarch, Mazu and Linji to whom was transmitted the Buddha's Dharma of the mind." He further praised me, saying, "The legacy of Seon will spread far and wide during your generation."

Then in the year of the Sheep (1967), Master Hyanggok ascended the high Dharma seat and prepared to give a Dharma talk at the closing ceremony for the summer retreat. I rose before the assembly, prostrated myself three times, and said: "Master, I do not want to ask about something the Buddha and patriarchs know. Would you please tell me instead what the Buddha and patriarchs do not know?"

Master Hyanggok replied, "Nine times nine is eighty-one."

"That is what the Buddha and patriarchs know."

"Six times six is thirty-six."

Upon hearing this, I bowed and departed. Master Hyanggok then descended from the Dharma seat.

The next day, I went to the master's room and asked again, "I do not ask about the Buddha eye or the correct Dharma eye. But, what is the correct Dharma eye of this patch-robed monk?"

Mater Hyanggok replied, "An old Buddhist nun congenitally performs woman's work."

"Today, I saw you in person for the first time," I replied. "For the last nine years, we stayed together but today, I peered into your enlightened secret. Ah-ha! So this is what it means!"

Master Hyanggok asked back, "And where did you see me?"

I shouted, "Kwan!"

With this answer, he then entrusted me with the Dharma lamp of the Linji lineage and bestowed on me a Dharma Transmission Verse.

> The great living truth of the Buddhas and Patriarchs (佛祖大活句),
> Can be neither given nor taken (無傳亦無受).
> Now I entrust this Dharma of living phrase to you (今付活句時),
> Whether you furl or unfurl the exhibit of truth is entirely up to you (收放任自在).

뉴욕 리버사이드 교회에서 법회를 마친 후 늦은 시간까지 차담 중인 참석 대중
Participants gathered after the Dharma Talk at NY Riverside Church

It was 1967 and I was 33 years old (The 79th Dharma descendant of the Buddha). This tradition has been transmitted from teacher to student for more than 2,500 years since the time of Sakyamuni Buddha.

Thus, I hope all of you will continuously cultivate this practice of Ganhwa Seon and shatter the *hwadu* of "What is your true self before you are born of your parents?" When the eye of wisdom opens, you will be able to guide all people to the truth.

About a hundred years ago, there was an enlightened Seon master in Korea named Mangong (1871~1946). One day, as he was sitting on the veranda chatting with several of his disciples, a bird took off from the eaves. Master Mangong asked, "How many miles will that bird fly in a day? If any of you have an answer, let's hear it." A little later, Master Bowol stood up and gave this really wonderful response, "The bird hasn't traveled even a couple of steps." What a splendid exchange of truth this was!

After Master Mangong entered paranirvana at Sudeoksa Temple, Master Gobong later became the new Senior Teacher. One day, he was about to ascend the Dharma Seat to give a talk when Master Geumo grabbed the hem of his robe and said, "Please say something before you ascend the Dharma Seat."

Master Gobong said, "Let go of my robe!"

Geumo asked him again, "Please say something before ascending the Dharma Seat."

"Let go of my robe!"

Forty years later, Master Hyanggok asked this mountain monk, "If you were Master Gobong, what would you have said?"

This mountain monk bellowed a thunderous "AUUK!" Master Hyanggok examined my response and said, "If you roar like that it will blind all the people."

"It is this humble monk's (Jinje)'s fault."

"It is this old monk's (Hyanggok)'s fault."

This is how dharma debates are carried out.

When Seon Master Gobong was asked to give them a word before ascending to the high Dharma seat, he should have responded to the request. When I shouted "Hal," it was in order to find out whether the monk requesting it had his own awakening experience or not. But, Seon Master Hyanggok corrected me by saying, "If you keep shouting out "Hal!" this way, you'll end up blinding everyone in the world." As such, a clear eyed enlightened master should be able distinguish the difference between right and wrong and provide the right answer. If a grand mountain blocks one's view, one may not become a guide. Only those with clear eyed enlightenment are qualified to guide others in Seon practice.

When I immediately accepted that I was at fault, I replied, "This is this humble monk's error." Then Seon Master

Hyanggok replied in grand style, "This is this old monk's error." What a splendid exchange of truth this was!

Ladies and gentlemen, please reflect carefully on this story!

One day, thirty or forty dedicated monks from all over Korea gathered at Mangwol-sa Monastery. They were determined to see their true natures and have a great awakening so they forbade themselves from leaving the monastery and entered into a period of fierce meditation. They appointed Yongseong Sunim (1846~1940) to be the resident Seon master; Seogu Sunim (1875~1958), who would later become the first head of the Jogye Order, was the senior Seon practitioner; and Unbong Sunim (1889~1944) acted as the leader of the meditation hall. When they were halfway through the 90-day retreat period, Master Yongseong climbed up on the high seat and challenged them with this splendid question: "My true appearance cannot be seen by any of the sages of past, present, or future, or by enlightened masters of all generations. Those of you in the assembly here today, where can you see this mountain monk's true appearance?"

Unbong Sunim then stood up and gave this definitive answer: "You've hidden your body inside a glass jar."

Without responding, Master Yongseong immediately descended from the high seat and returned to his residence. Forty years later Master Hyanggok asked me, "At that time, if you were Master Yongseong, how would you have responded to the answer, 'You've hidden your body inside a glass jar'?"

Master Hyanggok had the right wisdom eye to ask this question. The answer given by Master Yongseong was good, but Master Hyanggok must have thought differently to ask this mountain monk again. Thus, this mountain monk replied, "I would have said, 'A clear-eyed enlightened master has given a tremendous answer,' and then stepped down." Master Hyanggok praised my answer.

Ladies and gentlemen in attendance here at Riverside Church, how would you answer if you are asked, "My true appearance cannot be seen by any of the sages of past, present, or future, or by enlightened masters over many generations. Where can you see this mountain monk's true appearance?" If any of you can give me an answer, let's hear it!

One person rose from the assembly and called out,
"Seon Master!"

The Master replied, "Calling out for me is not correct."

"Heavens, Oh Heavens!"

The Master replied, "You would get thirty blows with this staff if you were closer!"

[There was a long silence, so the Master said:]

My answer is, "Attendant! Lock the door!"

Do you understand?

Ten years ago many innocent people died from the 9/11 attack. I would like to dedicate this Dharma speech to them.

All the sacrificed souls from the 9/11 attack!

Originally there is no birth or death. The four elements, earth, water, fire, and wind, fundamentally do not exist. Both the five elements and the spiritual world are actually empty. I hope you understand these truths through my Dharma talk. Let go all of your attachments, hate, and resentment and rest in peace forever.

What do you think?

**As the clouds lift from the mountaintop, the ridgeline appears,
Only the bright moon floats atop the waves in the sea.**

What is your True self?

Thank you very much.

[Hitting his staff on the high seat, the Master descended.]

반기문 UN 사무총장과 간화선의 세계 평화 기여에 관한 대담 후, 2012

Master Jinje, Supreme Patriarch of the Jogye Order of Korean Buddhism and
Ban Ki-moon, Secretary-General of the United Nations, after a conversation about the
expected contribution of Ganhwa Seon to world peace (New York, 2012)

UN 세계종교지도자모임
초청법회 법어

2012.10.4. 뉴욕UN별관 Church Center

세계종교지도자 여러분!

이렇게 만나 뵙게 되어 대단히 반갑습니다. 산승(山僧)을 위해 이처럼 귀중한 자리를 준비해주시고 초청해주신 여러분께 깊이 감사드리며, 훌륭한 분들과 함께 하게 되어 대단히 영광스럽게 생각합니다.

지금까지 여러분들께서 이끌어 오신 세계 여러 종교 간의 대화는 인류와 지구촌의 평화와 번영을 위한 정신적 토대요, 밝은 미래로 인도하는 희망이었습니다. 우리는 이러한 대화를 통해 지혜와 복을 나누어 기아와 질병, 차별과 억압, 자연재해와 환경오염 등의 난제로 가득한 지구촌을 선도하여 왔고 만인에게 평화를 꿈꾸게 하고 있습니다.

고통받는 이들을 돕고 병든 세상을 치유하는 것은 우리 종교인들이 존재하는 이유이며, 책임과 의무입니다. 우리가 이러한 문제들을 등한시한다면 진정한 종교인이라 할 수 없을 것입니다. 저 불안과 고통 속에서 신음하는 이웃들의 믿음과 신뢰가 없다면 우리 종교인들도 본분을 다할 수 없을 것입니다.

그러므로 지금처럼 앞으로도 우리 종교인들이 앞장서 일깨워주고 실천하는 모습을 보여야 합니다. 먼저 손을 내밀며, 먼저 베풀고, 먼저 보살펴서 굶주림과 병고에서 벗어나게 해야 합니다. 저들을 일깨워주어 반목과 싸움을 멈추게 하고 환경과 생태계를 회복하도록 해야 합니다.

이것이 바로 우리 모든 종교가 존재하고, 신뢰하고, 수행하는 이유이며 의무라고 믿습니다. 산승도 그 의무를 다하기 위해 한편으로는 만인에게 참선 수행법인 '간화선(看話禪)'을 널리 유포하고, 다른 한편으로는 구호단체와 환경단체 지원에 적극 나설 것입니다.

이제 인류는 굶주림·질병·전쟁 등과 같은 오래된 문제들뿐만 아니라, 지구를 잘 돌보지 않아 생겨난 새로운 난제(難題)에 직면하였습니다. 아시는 바와 같이, 지구촌은 지난 수천 년간의 변화보다 최근 이백 년 동안의 변화가 더 큽니다. 급기야 이제는 인류와 지구촌의 존폐를 걱정할 처지가 되고 말았습니다. 우리는 '지구와 자연은 우리의 조상들이 건강하고 깨끗하게 보존하기를 간곡히 기원하며 물려준 것'이라는 사실을 잊고 있습니다.

우리가 얼마나 서로 밀접하게 연관되어 있는지, 또한 우리가 사는 지구와 인류가 얼마나 연결되어 있는지를 하루빨리 깨달아야 합니다. 이 세상과 우리 이웃들이 없는 것을 상상조차 할 수 있겠습니까? 우리는 어디에서 와서 어디로 가야 할까요? 우리의 삶은 어디에서 끝나며 어디에서 새로 시작해야 할까요? 땅이 없다면 우리가 어떻게 걸을 수 있을까요?

그래서 산승은 일생토록 품어왔던 원력(願力)인 지구촌과 인류의 평화로운 미래를 위해 여러분과 하나가 되어 열과 성을 다하고자 합니다. 이러한 난제들 가운데 어떤 것들은 너무나 심각해서 돌이키기 힘들지도 모릅니다. 그러나 그 가운데 우리 인류가 지구촌의 행복한 미래를 위해 화합할 훌륭한 기회가 있다고 산승은 믿습니다.

간화선 수행을 통해서 우리는 '참나'를 찾을 수 있으며, 참나를 찾으면 이러한 난제들을 해결할 수 있습니다.

"불교의 간화선 수행이 이러한 난제들을 해결하는데 어떻게 도움이 될 수 있을까?"라고 물으실 분도 계실 것입니다.

불교는 지난 2,500여 년 동안 인류의 문화적, 정신적 발전에 지대한 공헌(貢獻)을 해 왔습니다. 그리고 1,600여 년 동안 부처님의 정통법맥(正統法脈)을 이어오고 있는 한국불교는, 지구촌의 물질문화에 대해 새로운 방향과 효과적인 패러다임을 제시하여 영구적인 세계 평화 실현을 목적으로 하고 있습니다.

여러분께서 아시는 바와 같이, 유네스코 헌장은 "전쟁은 인간의 마음 속에서 생기는 것이므로 평화의 방벽(防壁)을 세워야 할 곳도 인간의 마음 속이다"라는 구절로 시작하고 있습니다.

전쟁이 인간의 마음에서 비롯되었다면, 평화의 해결책도 또한 마음에서 시작될 것입니다. 지구촌의 평화와 화목과 평등, 건강한 생태환경은 인류 개개인이 마음을 닦는 수행을 통해 나와 남이 둘이 아니라 하나라는 사실을 인식함으로써 이룩될 수 있습니다. 또한 인간과 자연은 서로 상생의 관계라는 사실을 인식하며, 온 지구촌이 나와 더불어 한 몸이라는 사실을 깨달아야 합니다.

참나를 찾아 마음의 고향에 이르게 되면,
자연과 인류가 상생한다는 것을 깨닫기 때문에 인간의 탐욕을 충족시키기 위해 환경을 파괴하고 생태계의 질서를 무너뜨려 고통을 불러들이는 어리석음을 범하지 않게 됩니다.
참선을 통해 참나를 깨닫게 되면,
'나'는 '우리'가 되고, '이기심'이 '이타심'이 되며, '아만심'이 '자비심'이 되어, 모두가 기꺼이 이웃을 돕고 우리의 보금자리인 지구촌을 보살피게 됩니다.
참나를 찾아 마음의 고향에 이르게 되면,
'나는 옳고 너는 그르다'는 시비심이 없어지고, 어리석음이 사라져 크게 지혜로워지므로, 반목과 갈등 그리고 전쟁이 없어지게 됩니다. 그러면 자연히 평화로운 세상이 이루어지게 될 것입니다.
그러면 참나를 어떻게 찾을 수 있을까요?

저는 그 수행법인 간화선을 여러분께 소개하고자 합니다. 이 수행은 바닷물이 짜고 꿀이 달다는 것을 아는 사람이라면 누구라도 할 수 있습니다. 왜냐하면 이 수행은 각자의 직분이나, 시간과 장소에 구애받지 않고 일상생활과 종교생활을 하는 가운데 닦아나가는 것이기 때문입니다.

모든 사람이 부모로부터 이 몸뚱이를 받아서 지금 이렇게 "나다" 하며 살고 있습니다. 그러나 이 몸뚱이는 백 년 이내에 썩어서 한 줌 흙으로 돌아가므로 진정한 '참나'라고 할 수 없습니다. 그렇다면 어떻게 참나를 찾을 수 있겠습니까?

"부모에게 나기 전에 어떤 것이 참나인가?"

하고 간절히 의심하고 의심하는 것입니다. 이것을 일러 '화두(話頭)'라고 합니다.

이 화두를 챙기고 의심하기를 끊어짐 없도록 노력하다 보면, 문득 참의심이 시동 걸리게 됩니다. 참의심이 시동 걸리면 그때는 시간 가는 줄도 모르고, 보되 보는 것도 잊어버리고, 듣되 듣는 것도 잊어버리고, 몸뚱이도 다 잊어버리고 오로지 화두의심이라는 한 생각으로 삼매(三昧)에 빠지게 됩니다.

이렇게 며칠이고 몇 달이고 화두의심에 푹 빠져서 시간이 흐르고 흐르다가 홀연히 사물을 보는 찰나, 소리를 듣는 찰나에 화두가 박살이 나게 됩니다. 그러면 완전한 참나를 깨닫게 되고 마음의 고향에 이르게 되는 것입니다.

인간과 자연이 하나라는 사실뿐만 아니라 깨달음의 과정을 잘 보여주는 일화를 예로 들어 보겠습니다.

옛날 중국에 '소동파(蘇東坡)'라는 대문장가가 있었는데, 어느 날 세상의 문장과 재주, 식견이 별것이 아니라는 것을 깨닫고 이후로는 참선수행에 몰두했습니다.

하루는 노산 흥룡사에 상총(常聰) 선사라는 안목이 고준한 선지식이 계신다는 소문을 듣고 찾아가게 되었습니다.

선사께 삼배의 예를 올리고 말하기를,

"선사님의 법문을 들으러 왔습니다."

하니, 이에 상총 선사께서 물으셨습니다.

"그대는 어째서 유정설법(有情說法)만 들으려 하고 무정설법(無情說法)은 들으려 하지 않는고?"

소동파는 선사의 물음에 큰 충격을 받았습니다. '생각과 정이 있는 유정물뿐만 아니라, 산이나 바위나 나무 같은 무정물도 설법을 한다?'

이 충격적인 말씀에 의심이 깊게 사무치게 되었는데, 친견하고 일어나 말을 타고 집으로 돌아오면서 온몸과 온 마음이 이 의심으로 가득 차게 되었습니다.

말 등에 앉아 집으로 돌아오는 동안에 소동파는 한 생각에 깊이 빠져서 의심삼매(疑心三昧)에 든 것입니다. '어떻게 무정물이 진리를 설할 수 있는가? 왜 나는 그것을 듣지 못하는가?'

그렇게 수십 리 먼 길을 말을 타고 돌아가다가 산모퉁이를 도는 순간, 산골짜기에서 짚동 같은 폭포수가 떨어지는 소리에 크게 깨달아 마음의 고향을 보게 되었습니다.

그리하여 게송을 지었습니다.

산골짜기에 흐르는 물소리가 팔만 사천 지혜의 말씀인데
산색이 어찌 부처님의 청정한 몸이 아니겠는가!
밤이 옴에 팔만 사천 법문을
다른 날에 어떻게 사람에게 들어서 보일꼬.

계성자시광장설(溪聲自是廣長舌)인데
산색기비청정신(山色豈非淸淨身)이리오.
야래팔만사천게(夜來八萬四千偈)를
타일여하거사인(他日如何擧似人)하리오.

이후로 소동파는 마음의 고향에서 남은 생을 지혜롭고 안락하게 누리며 살았습니다.

대중 여러분!

우리는 불경과 성경과 코란 등 성전(聖典)뿐만 아니라 정(情)이 없는 저 돌덩이와 물과 자연도 한량없는 지혜의 말씀을 전하고 있다는 것을 알아야 합니다. 우리가 저 무정물이 설하는 진리의 말씀까지 들을 수 있을 때, 지구를 위협하는 생태적 위기와 환경문제에서 벗어나 지구촌은 진정한 평화를 맞이할 수 있을 것입니다.

세계의 모든 형제자매 여러분!

세계는 지금 극단적인 개인주의에서 비롯된 개인 간의 다툼, 사상의 충돌, 종교와 국가 그리고 인종 간의 갈등으로 위기로 치닫고 있습니다. 이 모두가 순수하게 보존되어야 할 우리 지구촌의 평화로운 환경을 위협하고 파괴해 왔습니다.

산은 모든 종류의 짐승들과 새들을 양육하고, 사람들에게 신선한 공기를 선사합니다.

물은 모든 고기와 어패류를 양육하며 인류와 무정에게 생명의 은인이 되니, 산과 물과 같은 덕행을 행하여 우리의 터전을 육성하고 보호해야 합니다.

온 세계는 하나입니다. 환경과 생태의 파괴는 곧 인류와 지구촌의 위기입니다. 왜냐하면, 만물은 나와 여러분과 더불어 둘이 아니기 때문입니다.

끝으로 인류와 지구촌이 지금의 생태적 위기에서 벗어나 영원한 평화와 행복 그리고 번영이 가득하기를 바라는 마음으로, 모든 분에게 산승이 직접 지은 게송 한 수를 선물해 드리고자 합니다.

향상과 향하의 진리의 일은 떼어놓기가 어려움이요,
뜻을 얻고 말을 잊어야사 진리의 도에 친함이라.

일구의 진리는 밝고 밝아 일만 가지 형상에 합함이요,
구월의 국화꽃은 새로움이로다.

향상향하사난분(向上向下事難分)이요
득의망언도이친(得意忘言道易親)이라.
일구명명해만상(一句明明該萬像)이요
중양구일국화신(重陽九日菊花新)이로다.

 귀한 시간을 내어 산승의 법문을 경청해 주신 여러분께 다시 한 번 감사드립니다.

미국 국가조찬기도회 60주년 행사에 참석하여 법문하시는 종정 예하, 2012

Master Jinje gives a Dharma Talk at the 60th National Prayer Breakfast in the US

World Peace and the Ecological Crisis: Buddhist Wisdom

October 4, 2012, UN sponsored World Religious Leaders Meeting, UN Plaza NYC

I would like to express my deepest gratitude to all who have invited me and prepared such a precious event. I am very honored to be among you.

This interreligious dialogue, for which all of you have worked hard, has been providing a spiritual foundation for peace and prosperity, as well as the hope for the future. Despite the world's problems of famine, disease, discrimination, oppression, environmental disasters, and environmental pollution, with the help of inter religious conversation, as well as sharing our wisdom and merit together, we still inspire people to dream of peace.

As religious leaders, our raison d'etre, our responsibility and duty, is to help those suffering and heal the world's ills. We are not truly religious if we do not address these issues. Without the belief and trust of neighbors, who are suffering in anxiety and pain, religious leaders can not be true to their calling.

We, as religious leaders, must awaken people and show them a model. We must give first, we must reach out our hands first, we must take care of others first in order to relieve hunger and sickness. We must awaken people to cease their fighting and hatred and restore the environment and the ecosystem.

I deeply believe that this is the reason that all religions exist. In order to fulfill these duties, this mountain monk will try to teach Ganhwa Seon practice while also starting to work with relief organizations and environmental groups.

We have not been good caretakers of the earth. The global changes observed in the last two hundred years are far greater than those that have occurred over the previous thousands of years. We do not know whether our planet or mankind can survive this new crisis or not. We almost forget that this earth, this nature has been handed down to us from our ancestors, with their special wish for us to keep it healthy and clean.

We must realize how interconnected we are with the earth and one another—with the earth that houses us with the human beings that make up our communities. Consider, where do we as individuals begin and end? Where do our lungs end and the air we breathe begin? How can we walk without the ground beneath our feet? I join you with my lifelong wish to work harder for the coming generations. Now, some of these changes, these challenges, are extremely detrimental and may even be irreversible. But in these challenges are great opportunities as well.

By practicing Ganhwa Seon, which is a way to transcend the false self, we discover the way to the true self. This is what must be taught—a way of meditation that uncovers the true self and provides a proper preparation and orientation for action.

"How can the Buddhist teachings of Ganhwa Seon meditation help?" you may ask. Buddhist teaching are ancient, going back more than 2,500 years and have contributed to human spiritual and cultural development. Korean Buddhism, since its inception 1,600 years ago, has followed the authentic Dharma lineage; it aims at establishing eternal world peace through a new paradigm, a fresh direction for our materialistic culture. This mountain monk thinks the time has come. Now is the right time.

As you well know, the UNESCO charter starts with this phrase, "That since wars begin in the minds of men, it is in the minds of men that the defenses of peace must be constructed." So if war begins in men's minds, solutions for peace begin there as well. Seon meditation teaches that global peace, harmony, and equality—as well as a healthy ecological environment—can be achieved by keeping our minds right and understanding that you and I are not two but one. We must also understand that this same "oneness" exists between the global habitat and the individual; human beings and nature are mutually interdependent.

When you find your true self and reach the home of your mind, you understand the mutual relationship between nature and human beings; there should be no environmental destruction and ecological damage inflicted only to satisfy the greed.

When you find your true self and reach home of your mind, then there will be no "I'm right, you're wrong." Ignorance will disappear and we will be filled with great wisdom. Confrontation, conflict and war will disappear and a peaceful world will naturally follow.

So how can we find our true selves then? I believe the answer lies in Ganhwa Seon practice, which I would like to share with you. It can be done by anyone who tastes seawater and says it is salty, or by anyone who tastes honey and says it is sweet. Because this practice is not restricted by individual character, time, or place, it can be performed during the normal daily life and spiritual life.

Everyone lives with a concept of "this is me" and "this is not me." But since this body dies, decays and returns to nature in less than a hundred years, the physical body can not be the "true self."

So how can you find your true self? Ask yourself this question, "What is my true self before I was born of my parents?" We have to ask this question again and again. This question is called a *hwadu*.

You have to question it sincerely, over and over again, putting great effort into questioning continuously. In this state, you will forget how much time passes, what you see or hear, even your own body. This single *hwadu* question will flow in an intense spiritual concentration called samadhi, with only the *hwadu*. You will be absorbed in *hwadu* samadhi for several days or even months. Then one moment when you see an object or hear a sound, your *hwadu* will suddenly shatter and you will find your true self, arriving at the home of your mind.

Let me illustrate process, as well as our innate ties with nature, with a story. In ancient China, there was a very famous writer named Su Dongpo. One day he realized the emptiness of all of his fame, talent, and thoughts, and so he decided to dedicate himself to Seon Practice. One day, he heard about the brilliant Master Changcong who taught at Xinglong Temple on Mt. Lushan and went to visit him.

After three formal bows, he said, "Master, I came to listen to your Dharma talk."

But Master Changcong asked him, "How is it that you can only hear the Dharma taught by people, yet you can not hear the Dharma taught by nature?"

Su Dongpo was astonished by the master's question. In addition to sentient beings with thoughts and emotions, can non-sentient objects like mountains, rocks, and trees also teach us the truth of dharma? The degree of his astonishment brought a great degree of doubt. As Su Dongpo left the temple and headed to his house, his mind went back to the master's words: "Nature teaches the Dharma?" This questioning filled his whole body as well as his whole mind.

While sitting on his horse's back, Su Dongpo entered the questioning Samadhi, the state of absolute and intense focus: "How can insentient objects teach the Truth? Why can't I hear it?" As his horse went around a corner, he heard the loud sound of a waterfall and he was enlightened; he saw the home of his mind! He wrote this verse of enlightenment:

> The roaring of the waterfall expounds 84,000 Buddha's teachings;
> How is this green mountain anything but the body of Buddha?
> In the dark night, the 84,000 teachings-
> How can I show them to everyone the next day?

After that, Su Dongpo enjoyed a blissful life of wisdom. So we must realize that not only the sacred scriptures like the Bible, Koran, and sutras but also nature, stones, and streams teach us truth and wisdom. Once we can hear the non-sentient, we will answer the problems of our ecological crisis that threatens our planet. Genuine world peace will follow.

Brothers and sisters everywhere, the world cries out for healing from radical individualism, which pits one individual against the other, ideology against ideology, and nation and religions against each other—all have threatened the integrity of our planetary environment.

Mountains nurture all kinds of animals and birds; they produce fresh air for people. Water is home to all kinds of fish and shellfish while providing life for plants and human beings. We must emulate the virtue of mountains, air, and water by nurturing and protecting our home.

The whole world is just one. We must not be seduced by delusion; because ten thousand different things are not separate from me, nor are they separate from you.

To end this speech, I would like to recite my poem. This is my prayer for eternal peace, happiness, and prosperity in our future.

> It is difficult to distinguish between
> The supreme truth and mundane truth.
> You must gain the meaning,
> Yet forget all words
> To come close to the truth.
> This one phrase of truth,
> Is bright – so bright – it is one with all phenomena.

Chrysanthemums bloom anew in autumn.

Thank you for taking the time to listen to my words today.

소참법문하시는 모습

Master Jinje giving a Dharma talk to a small group of monastics

인성교육 오계(人性敎育 五戒)

 현대사회는 기계화와 산업화로 경제가 발전하고 물질이 풍요로워졌지만, 정신세계는 도리어 빈한해졌습니다.

 사람들은 인생의 목적과 삶의 가치를 인간의 보편적 가치인 인성에 두지 않게 되었습니다. 이기적 물질만능주의에 매몰되어, 정신보다 물질적 가치만을 추구함으로써 인간다운 삶을 추구하는 정의와 도덕과 윤리의 정신세계는 피폐해지고 물질이 사회전반을 지배하게 되었습니다. 정신적 성숙 없이 물질만이 발전하는 것은 모래 위에 성을 쌓는 것처럼 허망한 것입니다.
 개인의 인격완성과 국가와 사회의 선진발전을 위해서는 청소년을 비롯하여 모든 국민이 인성교육을 통해서 인성을 회복해야 합니다.

 이에 산승(山僧)이 미래의 희망인 모든 청소년과 대중에게 인류의 밝은 내일을 위하여 다음과 같이 인성교육 오계(五戒) 사상을 제시합니다.

　인성교육의 목표가 되는 것으로, 정부에서는 여덟 가지를 그 가치 덕목으로 정하였으니 예(禮), 효(孝), 정직(正直), 책임(責任), 존중(尊重), 배려(配慮), 소통(疏通), 협동(協同)이 그것입니다.

　그 여덟 가지 덕목을 우리가 바르게 실천하는데 있어서 먼저, 인간의 기본조건인 신구의(身口意) 삼업(三業)을 청정하게 해야 합니다.
　인간의 기본행위인 생각과 말과 행동을 바르게 하며 인간의 기본 장애인 탐진치(貪瞋癡) 삼독을 제거하기 위하여 인간의 기본 과목인 계정혜(戒定慧) 삼학을 닦아야 합니다.
　계(戒)는 도덕 윤리를 잘 지키고 품행을 단정히 하는 것이고, 정(定)은 마음의 산란심을 없애기 위해 참선을 하는 것이며, 혜(慧)는 참선을 함으로써 지혜를 뚜렷이 밝히는 것입니다.
　참선은 '부모에게 나기 전에 어떤 것이 참나인가?'라는 화두를 오매불망 참구하는 데 있습니다.

　그 실천적 다섯 가지 덕목을 제시하니 다음과 같습니다.

첫째는 국가와 사회에 필요한 사람이 됩시다.

　사람들과의 관계에서 인성과 인간성이 좋아야 합니다.

인성(人性)은 사람이 타고난 본성을 말하고 인간성(人間性)은 사람의 도덕성을 말합니다. 인성과 인간성을 꾸준히 수양해 훌륭히 발전시켜서 어디서나 꼭 필요한 사람이 됩시다.

둘째는 부모와 조상님께 효도합시다.

부모와 조상님께는 공경하며 효도를 행합시다.
효도는 모든 행동의 근본이며 모든 선(善)은 효도에서부터 비롯합니다.
이 몸이 태어남에 부모와 조상님이 없다면 어찌 지금의 내가 태어남이 있겠습니까.
효는 백행의 근본(百行之根本)입니다.

셋째는 친구와 이웃을 사귐에 있어 서로 신의와 사랑으로 합시다.

대인관계에 있어서는 서로 예절을 갖추고 믿음이 있어야 합니다.
예절이 없는 아랫사람은 사랑을 받지 못하며, 윗사람은 아랫사람에게 도리와 염치가 있어야 합니다.
주변 친구에게는 신의와 의리가 있어야 하며, 이웃사촌들에게는 친절함으로 신뢰와 믿음의 공동체가 되어야 합니다.
인생에서 물질보다 가치 있는 것은 좋은 친구와 이웃을 두는 것입니다. 어려워할 때는 진심으로 도와주고, 힘들어할 때는 서로 위로해 주고, 좋은 일이 있을 때 함께 기뻐한다면, 인생은 향기롭고 세상은 아름다워집니다.

넷째는 맡은 바 일에 있어 성실과 정성을 다합시다.

세상에는 모두에게 각자의 일이 있습니다.
개인 개인이 자기의 일에 최선을 다한다면 서로에게 약속을 지키는 것입니다.
성실과 약속은 우리 사회의 주춧돌입니다

다섯째는 대자비심을 가지고 뭇 생명을 존중합시다.

이 세상에서 귀하고 소중한 것은 자신의 생명입니다.
'나만의 생각'에 갇힐 때 모든 갈등과 번뇌가 발생하고 그것이 충족되지 않을 때 평정심을 잃고 좌절하여 소중한 생명을 스스로 마감합니다.
참선수행을 하면 나만을 생각하는 것에서 벗어나게 되고 타인과 주변을 돌아보게 되어 삼라만상이 다 내 몸과 다름없음을 알게되어 풀 한 포기 미물 하나도 함부로 훼손하지 않습니다.
나를 아끼고 사랑하며 타인을 생각하며 살아있는 모든 생명을 존중합시다.

그리하여 우리 스스로가 더 나은 사회와 국가 인류를 위하여 말과 행동을 좌우하는 생각의 틀을 바꿉시다.

남을 의심하거나 무시하는 부정적 사고를 버리고, 상대를 믿고 사랑하는 긍정적 사고의 지혜인(智慧人)이 되어야 합니다.

사람은 다른 동물과 달리 예의와 염치가 있고 효도와 사랑을 합니다. 정직하고 책임감 있는 참사람이 되어 남의 인격과 생명을 존중하고 배려합시다. 항상 즐거운 대화로 소통하고 합심하여 건전한 국가 사회를 만듭시다.

모든 청소년이, 나아가 만인이 인생에서 기본이 되는 다섯 가지 계율을 잘 받들어 행한다면, 온 집안이 화목하고 인류사회가 다툼과 갈등이 없는 평화롭고 행복한 세상이 될 것입니다.

종정 예하에 대한 스님들의 고두례
광복 70주년 한반도 통일과 세계 평화를 위한 세계 간화선 무차대법회, 2015

Monastics offering "godurye" to Master Jinje as the last ritual of the three prostrations
The Conference for World Peace and Reunification of Korea - Great Equality Assembly of Ganhwa Seon (Seoul, 2015)

The Five Virtues Leading to Character Development

The contemporary world is one of materialism and great economic growth, but with decrease in spirituality.

With the extremes of such a materialistic world-view, people's ideals and life-goals have deviated far from the pursuit of human dignity and basic rights. People tend to neglect their spiritual well-being, perhaps blinded by the pursuit of selfish gain and material wealth. Modern society often seems to forget its sense of morality, justice and ethics. The world at times seems dominated by this materialistic outlook and its accompanying degradation of spiritual interests and pursuits.

Material progress without spiritual maturity is as futile as building a castle on sand.

We must seek to restore the moral character of our children

and citizens through a transformation in ethics. This will bring about individual development and the betterment of our society.

To accomplish this, the following five precepts of character development are proposed for our children, the hope of our future, and our citizens, to lead us into a brighter future.

The eight virtues for the development of character, as outlined by the Korean Government, are: proper decorum, filial piety, honesty, responsibility, respect, kind consideration, communication and cooperation.

Here's what we can do to practice these eight virtues.

First, to purify the three basic modes of human activity, which are the body, mind and speech, we must cultivate proper thinking, proper speech and proper conduct. To eradicate the three basic obstacles to humanity, which are greed, hatred and ignorance, we must cultivate the three basic virtues, ethics, concentration and wisdom.

Ethics refers to observing morality and proper conduct. Concentration refers to practicing meditation to avoid distractions of the mind. Wisdom refers to illuminating wisdom based on meditation practice.

In Seon meditation, one ceaselessly investigates a *hwadu*, such as "What is my true self before I was born of my parents?"

Here are the five virtues of learning to be maintained for life.

First,
Be a positive contribution to society.
In building human relationships, one must maintain a good character and nature. Human character is one's innate personality at birth, while human nature refers to one's ethical values developed through life. Cultivate both good character and good nature to be a valuable presence to all.

Second,
Honor your parents and respect your elders.
Piety forms the foundation of all deeds, and serves as the basis of Seon. Without one's parents and ancestors, how could there have been the birth of this body? Piety lays the foundation for a myriad of human actions.

Third,
Build worthy friendships in love and trust.

Pay respect to and confide in your elders and superiors.

It is difficult to receive the love of one's elders without respect. Elders must carry out their duties with honor.

Be loyal and respectful to your friends, and be kind to your neighbors. This builds a community of confidence and good faith.

Good friends and neighbors are more valuable than any material possession. Lend a hand to a friend in need, console a friend in hardship and rejoice together in times of good fortune. Standing together in good and bad times, your life will grow rich, and the world beautiful.

Fourth,
Be sincere and earnest in carrying out your responsibilities.
We each have work to do in this world. There is the bond of an oath in this.
In fulfilling our individual duty, we fulfill an oath to each other.
Sincere and earnest work forms the cornerstone of our society.

Fifth,
Respect all life with love and compassion.
Every person's life is important and valuable.

All conflicts and defilements arise from a narrow mind that thinks only of itself. Because selfish desires cannot be fulfilled, one becomes hopeless and without peace. This despair may lead one to end their own precious life.

In practicing Seon, one ceases to think only of their self and considers others. When you realize that the life of another is equal to your own, you cannot destroy even a single blade of grass nor any other seemingly insignificant creature. Be kind to yourself and show concern for others through love and respect for life.

For the betterment of our society, nation and world, we must break the mold that forms our way of thinking, which in turn affects our speech and actions.

Rather than indulging in pessimistic views of suspicion and disrespect, seek out the wisdom of optimism, love and trust.

In contrast to other forms of life, humans show respect and honor, and display love and piety. As a human being, through honesty and responsible conduct, respect the lives of others and communicate through joy and unity in order to build a healthy society.

When our children and all of humanity practice the five precepts, there will be harmony in our families and this will become a world of joy and peace, without war and conflict.

전법(傳法)의 원류(源流)

부처님으로부터 내려오는 심인법(心印法)이 한 가닥 우리나라에 남아있으니, 한국 선맥의 중흥조(中興祖)이신 경허(鏡虛) 선사로부터 혜월(慧月) 선사, 운봉(雲峰) 선사, 향곡(香谷) 선사 그리고 산승(山僧)에 이르기까지의 전법게(傳法偈)와 전수(傳受)했던 과정을 밝히노라.

전법게-향곡 선사가 진제 선사에게

The Dharma Transmission Verse given to Master Jinje by Master Hyanggok

혜월혜명(慧月慧明)스님은 동진으로 출가하여 경허(鏡虛) 선사로부터 화두를 타서 불철주야 공부를 지어가길 3년이란 세월이 지난 어느 날, 짚신 한 켤레를 다 삼아놓고서 잘 고르기 위해 신골을

치는데, '탁'하는 소리에 화두가 타파되었다.

그 길로 경허 선사를 찾아가니, 경허 선사께서 물음을 던지셨다.

"목전(目前)에 고명(孤明)한 한 물건이 무엇인고?"

이에 혜명스님이 동쪽에서 몇 걸음 걸어서 서쪽에 가서 서니, 경허 선사께서 다시 물으셨다.

"어떠한 것이 혜명(慧明)인가?"

"저만 알지 못할 뿐만 아니라 일천 성인(聖人)도 알지 못합니다."

이에 경허 선사께서

"옳고, 옳다!"

하시며 인가(印可)하시고, '혜월(慧月)'이란 법호(法號)와 함께 상수제자(上首弟子)로 봉(封)하시고 전법게(傳法偈)를 내리셨다.

[임인년, 서기1902년][석가여래부촉법 제76법손]

혜월 혜명에게 부치노니,

일체법(一切法)을 요달해 알 것 같으면

자성에는 있는 바가 없는 것.

이같이 법성을 깨쳐 알면

곧 노사나불을 보리라.

세상법에 의지해서 그릇 제창하여

문자와 도장이 없는 도리에 청산을 새겼으며

고정된 진리의 상에 풀을 발라 버림이로다.

부 혜월혜명(付 慧月慧明)

요지일체법(了知一切法)하면

자성무소유(自性無所有)라.

여시해법성(如是解法性)하면

즉견노사나(卽見盧舍那)라.

의세제도제창(依世諦倒提唱)하여

무문인청산각(無文印靑山脚)하며

일관이상도호(一關以相塗糊)로다.

수호 중춘 하한일(水虎 仲春 下澣日)
만화문인 경허 설함(萬化門人 鏡虛 說)

운봉성수(雲峰性粹)스님은 동진(童眞)으로 출가하여 경율(經律)을 모두 섭렵하였는데 거기에서 만족을 얻지 못하고, '대오견성법(大悟見性法)이 있다는데 나도 도인(道人)이 되어야겠다'는 생각으로 남방의 위대한 선지식이신 혜월 선사를 찾아가서 열심히 참구(參究)하였지만, 10여 년이 지나도 순일(純一)함을 이루지 못하였다. 그래서 오대산 적멸보궁(寂滅寶宮)에 가서 백일기도를 올리며, '화두일념이 현전하고 견성대오하여 종풍을 드날려 광도중생하여지이다' 하며 지극한 마음으로 발원을 드렸다.

백일기도를 회향하고 백양사(白羊寺) 운문암(雲門庵)에서 불철주야 정진한 끝에 타성일편(打成一片)을 이루어, 어느 날 새벽 선방문을 열고 나오는데, 밝은 달에 온 산하대지(山河大地)가 환하게 밝은 것을 보고 활연대오(豁然大悟)하였다.

그리하여 오도송을 읊었다.

문을 열고 나서자 갑작스레 찬 기운이 뼛골에 사무침에
가슴 속에 막혔던 물건 활연히 사라져 버렸네.
서릿바람 날리는 밤에 객들은 다 돌아갔는데
단청 누각은 홀로 섰고 빈 산에는 흐르는 물소리만 요란하더라.

출문맥연한철골(出門驀然寒徹骨)하니
활연소각흉체물(豁然消却胸滯物)이라.
상풍월야객산후(霜風月夜客散後)에
채누독재공산수(彩樓獨在空山水)로다.

그리하여 그 당시 부산 선암사에 계시던 혜월(慧月) 선사를 참방(參訪)하여 여쭈었다.

"삼세제불(三世諸佛)과 역대조사(歷代祖師)는 어느 곳에서 안심입명(安心立命)하고 계십니까?"

이에 혜월 선사께서 양구(良久)하시므로, 스님이 냅다 한 대 치면서,

"산 용이 어찌 죽은 물에 잠겨 있습니까?"

하니, 혜월 선사께서 도리어 물으셨다.

"그러면 너는 어찌 하겠느냐?" 이에 성수스님이 문득 불자(拂子)를 들어 보이니, 혜월 선사께서는

"옳지 못하고 옳지 못하다"

하시며 부정하셨다. 그러니 스님이 다시 응수하기를,

"스님, 기러기가 창문 앞을 날아간 지 이미 오래입니다."

라고 하자, 혜월 선사께서 크게 한바탕 웃으시며,

"내 너를 속일 수가 없구나!"

하시고 매우 흡족해 하셨다.

그리하여 을축년에 '운봉(雲峰)'이라는 법호와 함께 상수제자로 봉하시고 전법게를 내리셨다.

[을축년, 서기 1925년][석가여래부촉법 제77법손]

운봉 성수에게 부치노니,

일체의 유위법(有爲法)은

본래 진실된 모양이 없으니

저 모양 가운데 모양이 없으면

곧 이름하여 견성(見性)이라 함이라.

부 운봉성수 (付 雲峰性粹)

일체유위법(一切有爲法)은

본무진실상(本無眞實相)이니

어상약무상(於相若無相)이면

즉명위견성(卽名爲見性)이라.

세존응화 2951년 4월(世尊應化 二九五一年 四月)
경허문인 혜월 설함(鏡虛門人 慧月 說)

이후 제방에서 납자(衲子)를 제접(提接)하시며 선의 종지(宗旨)를 크게 펼치시니, 도법(道法)의 성황함이 당대의 으뜸이셨다.

향곡혜림(香谷蕙林)스님은 16세 때, 스님이었던 형님을 만나러 어머니와 함께 운봉(雲峰) 선사께서 조실로 계시는 천성산(千聖山) 내원사(內院寺)에 가게 되었다. 그 때 많은 스님들이 모여서 참선(參禪)을 하는 광경을 보고는 모친만 집으로 되돌아가시게 하고는 운봉 선사로부터 화두를 타서 공양주를 2년간 하면서 공부하였다.

그러던 어느 봄날에 산골짜기에서 바람이 불어와 열어놓은 문이 왈카닥 닫히는 소리에 마음의 경계가 있어, 운봉 선사를 찾아갔다. 조실방을 들어서는 그 모습이 당당하니, 선사께서 이미 가늠하시고 목침(木枕)을 내밀어 놓고,

"한 마디 일러라!"

하시거늘, 혜림스님이 즉시에 목침을 발로 차버리니, 선사께서

"다시 일러라!"

하셨다. 이에 혜림스님이

"천언만어(千言萬語)가 다 몽중설몽(夢中說夢)이라. 모든 불조(佛祖)가 나를 속였습니다."

하였다. 이에 운봉 선사께서 크게 기뻐하시었다.

그리하여 신사년 8월에 '향곡(香谷)'이란 법호와 함께 상수제자로 봉하시고 전법게를 내리셨다.

〔신사년, 서기 1941年〕[석가여래 부촉법 제78법손]

향곡 혜림 장실에게 부치노니,
서쪽에서 온 문인(文印)이 없는 진리는
전할 수도 받을 수도 없나니,
만약 전하고 받을 수 없는 것조차 여의면
까마귀는 날고 토끼는 달리느니라.

부 향곡혜림 장실(付 香谷蕙林 丈室)
서래무문인(西來無文印)은
무전역무수(無傳亦無受)라
약리무전수(若離無傳受)하면
오토부동행(烏兎不同行)이라.

세존응화 2967년(世尊應化 二九六七年)
혜월문인 운봉 설함(慧月門人 雲峰 說)

그리하여 임제정맥(臨濟正脈)의 법등(法燈)을 상속 부촉하여 가시니, 즉 임제(臨濟), 양기(楊岐), 밀암(密庵), 석옥(石屋), 태고(太古), 환성(喚惺), 율봉(栗峰), 경허(鏡虛)의 적전(嫡傳)이다.

향곡 선사께서는 그 후 정해년(丁亥年)에 문경 봉암사(鳳巖寺)에서 도반들과 정진하던 중,

죽은 사람을 죽여 다하여야만 산 사람을 보고,
죽은 사람을 살려 다하여야만 비로소 죽은 사람을 보게 될 것이다.

살진사인(殺盡死人)하야사 방견활인(方見活人)이요
활진사인(活盡死人)하야사 방견사인(方見死人)이라.

라는 고인(古人)의 법문을 들면서 "일러보라!"는 한 도반의 말에 삼칠일 동안 침식을 잊고 일념삼매(一念三昧)에 들었다가, 홀연히 자신의 양손이 흔들리는 것을 보고 활연대오(豁然大悟)하셨다.

홀연히 두 손을 보니 전체가 드러났네.
삼세제불도 눈(眼) 속의 꽃이로다.
천경만론(千經萬論)은 이 무슨 물건인가?
이로 좇아 불조(佛祖)가 모두 몸을 잃어버렸도다.
봉암사에 한 번 웃음은 천고의 기쁨이요,
희양산 굽이굽이 만겁에 한가롭도다.
내년에 다시 한 수레바퀴 밝은 달이 있어서

금풍(金風: 가을바람)이 부는 곳에 학의 울음 새롭구나.

홀견양수전체활(忽見兩手全體活)이라.
삼세불조안중화(三世佛祖眼中花)로다.
천경만론시하물(千經萬論是何物)인고?
종차불조총상신(從此佛祖總喪身이로다.
봉암일소천고희(鳳巖一笑千古喜)요
희양수곡만겁한(曦陽數曲萬劫閑)이로다.
내년갱유일륜월(來年更有一輪月)하야
금풍취처학려신(金風吹處鶴唳新)이로다.

이후부터 천하 노화상(老和尙)의 설두(舌頭)에 속임을 입지 않고 임운등등(任運騰騰), 등등임운(騰騰任運)하여 제방(諸方)에 대사자후(大獅子吼)를 하시었다.

산승(眞際法遠)은 불공드리러 절에 자주 다니던 친척을 따라서 동네에서 십 리쯤 떨어진 곳에 있던 해관암(海觀庵)이라는 조그마한 사찰에 우연히 갔다가, 석우(石友) 선사를 친견(親見)한 것이 출가의 인연이 되었다.

그리하여 1954년에 석우 선사께서 해인사 조실로 추대되심에 모시고 같이 가서 시봉하다가 그 해 사미계를 받았다.

그런 후로 다시 초대 종정으로 추대되시니, 동화사로 거처를 옮기어 모시게 되었다. 1957년(세수 24세)에 석우 선사께 '부모미생전 본래면목(父母未生前本來面目)' 화두를 받아 선문(禪門)에 들어서 운수행각(雲水行脚)의 길에 올랐는데, 일거일동 화두와 씨름해서 '일념삼매(一念三昧)만 되면 대오견성한다'는 그 확신을 받아들여 밤낮으로 씨름하였다.

 한철은 선산 도리사에서 일고여덟 분의 수좌(首座) 스님들과 동안거(冬安居)를 나게 되었는데, 밤 9시가 되어 방선하면 잠시 누웠다가 대중이 모두 잠든 후에 조용히 일어나 두 세 시간 포행정진하며 하루하루를 빈틈없이 정진하였다. 그러다가 어느 날 그곳에서 참선 도중에 반짝 떠오르는 조그마한 지견(知見)을 가지고서 '알았다'는 잘못된 소견을 갖게 되어, 참구하던 것을 다 놓아 버리고는 해제일만 기다렸다.

 그러던 중 초대 종정이시던 석우 선사께서 열반(涅槃)에 드셨다는 부고(訃告)가 날아오니, 동화사로 가 다비(茶毘)를 치르고, 경남 월내(月內) 묘관음사(妙觀音寺)에 주석하고 계시던 향곡(香谷) 선사를 찾아갔다.

 찾아가니, 향곡 선사께서 대뜸,

 "일러도 삼십 방(三十棒)이요, 이르지 못해도 삼십 방이니 어떻게 하려느냐?"하셨다. 산승이 말을 못 하고 우물쭈물하자, 향곡 선사께서 다시 물으셨다.

 "남전(南泉) 선사의 참묘(斬猫)법문 가운데 '조주(趙州) 선사께서 신발을 머리에 이고 나가신 것'에 대해서 한 마디 일러 보아라."

　산승은 여기서도 바른 답을 하지 못하였다.
　이에 곧장 물러나와 2년 여 세월이 흐른 26세 때, 오대산(五臺山) 상원사(上院寺)에서 7,8명 선객스님들과 동안거(冬安居) 정진을 하던 중, 유달리 포근한 날이 있어 남쪽 마루에 앉아 문득 자신을 반조(反照)해 보게 되었다.
　'내가 정말로 견성을 했느냐? 견성을 했으면 일일법문(一一法問)에 전광석화(電光石火)와 같이 바로 바른 답이 나와야 되거늘 왜 그렇지 못하는가? 내가 나를 속여서야 되겠느냐! 이것은 큰 잘못 됨이 있으니 내가 이 소견을 가지고 만족을 한다면 아무 쓸 곳이 없도다. 백지 상태에서 다시 출발해야겠다. 나를 속이고 모든 이를 속이면 죄가 이만저만 아니다.'
　하고 스스로 반성하게 되었다. 여기에서 '알았다'하는 것을 모두 놓고, 해제하자마자 문답 과정에서 언하(言下)에 '옳다, 그르다' 칼질하셨던 향곡 선사 회상(會上)을 찾아갔다. 그리하여 향곡 선사께 예를 올리고,
　"이 일을 마칠 때까지 스님을 의지해서 공부하려고 왔습니다. 화두를 하나 내려주십시오."
　하고 말씀드리니, 향곡 선사께서
　"이 어려운 관문(關門)을 네가 어찌 해결할 수 있겠느냐? 못한다!"
　하시니, 다시 분명히 선을 그어 말씀드렸다.

"신명(身命)을 다 바쳐서 해보겠습니다. 이 관문을 뚫기 전에는, 다시는 바랑지고 산문(山門)을 나가지 않겠습니다."

이에 향곡 선사께서 '향엄상수화(香嚴上樹話)' 화두를 하나 내려 주시니, 일체 산문을 벗어나지 않고 공부하게 되었다.

어떤 사람이 아주 높은 나무 위에서 입으로만 나뭇가지를 물고 손으로 가지를 잡거나 발로 가지를 밟지도 않고 매달려 있을 때, 나무 밑에서 지나가는 이가 달마스님이 서역에서 중국으로 오신 뜻(祖師西來意)을 묻는데 있어서, 대답하지 않으면 묻는 이의 뜻에 어긋나고, 만약 대답한다면 수십 길 낭떠러지에 떨어져서 자기 목숨을 잃게 될 것이다. 이러한 때를 당하여 어찌해야 되겠느냐?

그리하여 이 화두를 들고 2년 여 동안 생사를 떼어 놓고 공부하였는데, 드디어 28세 때 가을에, 새벽에 예불 드리러 올라가다가 마당의 돌부리에 걸려 넘어져 일어나는 차제에 화두가 해결되니, 동문서답(東問西答)하던 종전의 미(迷)함이 걷혀지고 비로소 진리의 세계에 문답의 길이 열리게 되었다.

그리하여 오도송(悟道頌)을 지어 향곡 선사께 바치기를,

이 주장자 이 진리를 몇 사람이나 알꼬?
과거, 현재, 미래의 모든 부처님도 다 알지 못함이로다.
한 막대기 주장자가 문득 금빛 용이 되어서

한량없는 용의 조화를 마음대로 부림이로다.

자개주장기인회(這箇拄杖幾人會)아.
삼세제불총불식(三世諸佛總不識)이라.
일조주장화금룡(一條拄杖化金龍)이니
응화무변임자재(應化無邊任自在)로다.

하니, 향곡 선사께서 앞 구절은 묻지 아니하고 뒷 구절을 들어서 물음을 던지셨다.

"용이 홀연히 금시조(金翅鳥)를 만난다면, 너는 어떻게 하겠느냐?"

"당황하여 몸을 움츠리고 세 걸음 물러가겠습니다(屈節當胸退身三步)." 이렇게 산승이 답하니, 향곡 선사께서는

"옳고, 옳다!"

하시며 크게 기뻐하셨다. 이로 좇아 모든 법문의 문답을 척척 주고받음이 막힘이 없었는데, 오직 마조(馬祖) 선사의 '일면불월면불(日面佛月面佛)' 공안에만 다시 막혔다.

마조 선사께서 편찮으셔서 원주(院主)가 아침마다 문안을 드리기를,

"큰스님, 밤새 존후(尊候)가 어떠하십니까?"

하고 말씀드리니, 하루는 대뜸,

"일면불월면불이니라." 하셨다.

그래서 또다시 5년여 동안 전력(全力)을 다 쏟아 참구함으로써 해결되어 오도송(悟道頌)을 읊었다.

한 몽둥이 휘둘러 비로정상을 거꾸러뜨리고
벽력 같은 일 할로써 천만 갈등을 문대버림이로다.
두 칸 띠암자에 다리 펴고 누웠으니
바다 위 맑은 바람 만년토록 새롭도다.

일봉타도비로정(一棒打倒毘盧頂)하고
일할말각천만측(一喝抹却千萬則)이라.
이간모암신각와(二間茅庵伸脚臥)하니
해상청풍만고신(海上淸風萬古新)이로다.

그 후 산승이 33세이던 정미년 하안거 해제법회일에 묘관음사 법당에서 향곡 선사께서 법문을 하시기 위해 법상(法床)에 오르셔서 좌정(坐定)하시고 계시는 차제에, 산승이 나아가서 예삼배(禮三拜)를 올리고 여쭈었다.
"불조(佛祖)께서 아신 곳은 여쭙지 아니하거니와, 불조께서 아시지 못한 곳을 선사님께서 일러 주십시오."
"구구(九九)는 팔십일(八十一)이니라."
"그것은 불조(佛祖)께서 다 아신 곳입니다." "육육(六六)은 삼십육(三十六)이니라." 이에 산승이 아무 말 없이 선사께 예배드리고 물러가니, 향곡 선사께서도 아무 말 없이 법상(法床)에서 내려오셔서 조실방(祖室房)으로 돌아가셨다.

뒷날 선사님을 찾아가서 예를 갖추고 다시 여쭈었다.

"불안(佛眼)과 혜안(慧眼)은 여쭙지 아니하거니와, 어떤 것이 납승(衲僧)의 안목(眼目)입니까?" "비구니 노릇은 원래 여자가 하는 것이니라(師姑元來女人做)."

"금일에야 비로소 선사님을 친견하였습니다." 이에 향곡 선사께서 물으셨다.

"네가 어느 곳에서 나를 보았는고?"

"관(關)!"

산승이 이렇게 답하자, 향곡 선사께서

"옳고, 옳다!" 하시며, 임제정맥(臨濟正脈)의 법등(法燈)을 부촉(付囑)하시고 '진제(眞際)'라는 법호와 함께 전법게를 내리셨다.

[정미년, 서기1967][석가여래부촉법 제79법손]

진제법원 장실에 부치노니,

부처님과 조사의 산 진리는

전할 수도 받을 수도 없는 것이라.

지금 그대에게 활구법을 부촉하노니

거두거나 놓거나 그대 뜻에 맡기노라.

부 진제법원 장실(付 眞際法遠 丈室)

불조대활구(佛祖大活句)는

무전역무수(無傳亦無受)라.

금부활구시(今付活句時)에

수방임자재(收放任自在)로다.

세존응화 2993년 8월 10일(世尊應化 二九九三年 八月 十日)

　　　　　　운봉문인 향곡 설함(雲峰門人 香谷 說)

Lineage of Seon Transmission

A thread of the Dharma transmitted directly from the Buddha himself is only alive in Korea. This is the lineage that Master Gyeongheo, who revived the Seon tradition in Korea, passed on to Master Hyewol, then to Master Unbong, who passed it on to Master Hyanggok, who then passed it to Master Jinje, the current Supreme Patriarch of the Jogye Order of Korean Buddhism. The circumstances of their Dharma transmissions are recorded here along with their Dharma transmission verses.

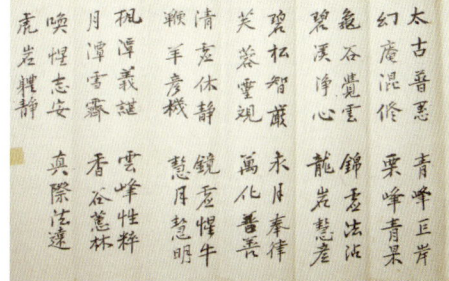

등등상속(燈燈相續) -
태고보우에서 진제법원까지 전승한 법맥

Deungdeung Sangsok: The document that certifies the lineage of Dharma transmission beginning from Taego Bou and leading to Jinje Beopwon

Seon Master Hyewol Hyemyeong (慧月慧明: bright light of wisdom) entered the monastery as a young boy. One day, he sought an audience with Master Gyeongheo and requested a *hwadu*. Master Gyeongheo obliged and he then considered this *hwadu* fervently, wrestling with it for over three years. One day, when Hyemyeong was making straw sandals, he put a shoe last into an almost completed sandal and struck it with a hammer. The loud sound. "Thwack!" shattered his *hwadu*.

Hyemyeong immediately went to see Master Gyeongheo, who asked him, "What is this one thing that is bright and clear in front of your eyes?"

Hyemyeong replied by walking from the east to the west a few steps, stopping in front of Master Gyeongheo.

"What is Hyemyeong then?"

Hyemyeong replied, "Not just me, none of the sages knows it either!"

"You are right, you are right!" Master Gyeongheo replied. Master Gyeongheo then conferred on him his seal of approval, gave him the new Dharma name Hyewol, and bestowed upon him a Dharma Transmission Verse. This happened in 1902, the Year of the Tiger.

Entrustment to Hyewol Hyemyeong

If you fully penetrate all Dharmas,

You see the non-beingness of self nature.

Like this, if you awaken to your Dharma nature,

You will soon see Vairocana Buddha.

Teaching false views by relying on worldly doctrines

Is to carve a blue mountain on the truth that has no letters or stamp,

Or to smear glue on the fixed form of the truth.

Seon Master Unbong Seongsu (雲峰性粹) became a monk as a young boy and eventually mastered both the sutras and the vinaya, but he still felt something was lacking. One day, he thought, "I heard there is a path that leads to great enlightenment and the attainment of one's True Self. I must become a sage too!" He then traveled to see the great southern sage, Seon Master Hyewol. After meeting Master Hyewol, he received his *hwadu* and practiced diligently for ten years, but his single-minded focus on questioning his *hwadu* did not flow purely and unceasingly. Therefore, he went to a sacred temple on Mt. Odae where a relic of the Buddha was enshrined. There he prayed ardently for one hundred days with the following aspiration: "May my *hwadu* single-mindedness flow unbroken.

May I attain great enlightenment so that the Seon tradition will flourish and all sentient beings may be guided and saved from suffering." He prayed for this every day with all his heart.

After completing one hundred days of prayer, Seongsu went to Unmun-am (雲門庵) Hermitage at Baegyang-sa (白羊寺) Temple for a retreat. He practicied fervently day and night until he finally reached a state where he and his *hwadu* became one. Early one morning, he opened the door of the Seon room to exit and saw the vast expanse of nature before him, the mountains and brooks beautifully illuminated by the moon. At that moment, he had a great awakening and recited this enlightenment verse:

> Upon opening a door, the cold instantly bites to the bone
> And makes that which formerly gripped my heart
> suddenly disappear.
> At dawn, when the frosty winds blow, the visitors are all gone.
> The painted pavilion stands alone, and the empty mountain is
> Filled only with the sound of a running stream.

To have his enlightenment confirmed, Seongsu went to Master Hyewol. After paying his respects, Seongsu said, "I ask about the Buddhas of the past, present and future, and of all the patriarchs. Where do they rest their minds and bodies?"

Master Hyewol just sat quietly. So Seongsu asked again, "Why is it that a living dragon remains immersed in dead water?"

"What would you do?" the Master asked back.

In response Seongsu held up a whisk, but the Master answered, "No, it is not!"

"Master" Seongsu then replied, "It has already been a long time since the geese flew by the window."

"I cannot fool you!" the Master admitted.

Master Hyewol was very satisfied. He entrusted Seongsu with the Dharma of the Linji lineage, gave him the Dharma name Unbong, and bestowed on him a Dharma transmission verse. This happened in 1925, the Year of the Ox.

Entrustment to Unbong Seongsu

All Dharmas that exist and cease to exist
Originally have no true form.
To realize that all phenomena are formless
Is to see their true nature.

One day, Seon Master Hyanggok Hyerim (香谷蕙林), went with his mother to visit his older brother, who was a monk at Naewon-sa (內院寺) Temple on Mt. Cheonseong. Deeply inspired after seeing dozens of monks in solemn practice, the future master told his mother to return home without him and joined the monastic order right away. He was sixteen years old.

Hyanggok received a *hwadu* from Master Unbong, the senior teacher at Naewon-sa Temple, which he wrestled with for two years while working in the temple kitchen. One spring day, he was concentrating on his practice after work while the doors to his room were open. Suddenly, the wind blowing from the valley slammed the doors shut with a loud "Bang," and he immediately attained a degree of awakening. He went directly went to see Master Unbong. When the Master saw this young monk walking confidently into the room, he knew there was something special about him. The Master pushed toward him the wooden pillow lying by his side and said, "Speak! Speak!" Hyanggok immediately kicked the wooden pillow away.

But Master Unbong kept urging him to answer: "Not correct! Speak again!" Hyanggok answered, "Thousands and tens of thousands of words are nothing but nocturnal ramblings! The Buddhas and sages of all ages have deceived me." Upon hearing this. Master Unbong was greatly overjoyed. In August 1941 Master Unbong gave him another Dharma name, Hyanggok, made him his head disciple, and bestowed on him a Dharma Transmission Verse. This happened in 1941, the Year of the Snake.

Entrustment to Hyanggok Hyerim

Truth from the west that has no letters or stamp
cannot be given or taken.
If liberated even from that which cannot be given or taken,
The crow flies, and the rabbit runs.

In this way, the Dharma of the Linji lineage was authentically transmitted without interruption. The lineage that had originated from Linji (臨濟) was passed on to Yangqi (楊岐), to Mian (密庵), to Shiwu (石屋), to Taego (太古), to Hwanseong (喚惺), to Yulbong (栗峰), and to Gyeongheo (鏡虛).

Later, in 1947, Master Hyanggok was practicing earnestly with fellow monks when one asked him, "A sage of the past said, 'You must kill a dead man completely to see the living, and revive a dead man completely to see the dead?' Do you understand the meaning of this?" For 21 days Master Hyanggok was totally absorbed in single-minded focus on this *hwadu* until he suddenly had a great awakening when he observed his two hands swinging as he walked. He then sang this enlightenment verse:

> Suddenly seeing two hands, the whole is revealed.
> All Buddhas of the past, present and future are
> Nothing but puppets in the eyes.
> Thousands of scriptures and ten thousand theories,
> What kind of a thing are they?
> Because of these scriptures and theories, all Buddhas and patriarchs lost their bodies.
> One laugh at Bongam-sa Temple is eternal happiness,
> Idyllic are the winding folds of Mt. Huiyang over 10,000 kalpas.
> The bright wheel of the moon will come again next year,
> The crane cries anew where the golden autumn wind blows.

From then on, Master Hyanggok was never fooled by the skillful words of old masters. He acted naturally like a flowing river and uttered a lion's roar as he traveled to many Seon monasteries.

Master Jinje entered monastic life sometime after he met his teacher Seon Master Seogu Bohwa (石友普化), at a small hermitage called Haegwan-am, about two miles from his home. He visited this hermitage with a relative who often went there to attend Buddhist services.

When Seon Master Seogu was invited to be the Most Senior Teacher of Haein-sa Monastery in 1954, Master Jinje followed him there to serve him and received the novice precepts that same year. Later, Seon Master Seogu was appointed the first Supreme Patriarch of the Jogye Order and moved to Donghwa-sa Monastery, where Master Jinje continued to serve as his attendant. While there, Master Jinje was initiated into Seon practice when Master Seogu gave him the *hwadu*, "What is your true self before you are born of your parents?" Thereafter, he practiced at many Seon centers, wandering like clouds and rivers. During a three month winter retreat at Dori-sa Temple with seven or eight other practitioners, he had a small spark of insight. From this, he deluded himself into thinking, "I have seen the truth." He then stopped investigating his *hwadu* altogether and just waited for the end of the retreat. Before the retreat ended, he received a notice that Master Seogu, had passed away. So he went back to Donghwa-sa and participated in his funeral ceremony.

Afterward, Master Jinje visited Master Hyanggok, who was presiding at Myogwaneum-sa. Upon seeing him, Master Hyanggok said abruptly, "I will give you 30 blows if you speak correctly, and I will still give you 30 blows if you don't speak correctly. What will you do?" Master Jinje didn't know what to say and hesitated. Master Hyanggok later tested him again by quoting another *gongan* where in Master Nanquan cuts a cat in two.

Master Hyanggok asked Master Jinje, "Speak about Master Zhaozhou's response where he put his sandals on his head and left the room when asked to give an answer about Master Nanquan's holding up the cat." Again, Master Jinje was not able to give a correct answer.

Master Jinje left at once. When he was 26 years old, after wandering for more than two years to many Seon monasteries, he spent a three-month winter retreat at Sangwon-sa Monastery on Mt. Odae-san. While there, he decided to let go of his illusion of having seen the truth. At the end of the winter retreat, he visited Master Hyanggok who gave him the *hwadu*, "Xiangyan

Goes Up a Tree."

Master Jinje studied this *hwadu* for over two years without leaving the mountain temple. Then one autumn day when he was 28 years old, the *hwadu* was finally shattered. All the wrong answers he had previously given were now resolved, and a path of dialogue with the truth was opened.

So he composed a poem and offered it to Master Hyanggok:

How many people have known the truth of this Dharma staff?
None of the Buddhas of the past, present or future know.
Suddenly this Dharma staff transforms into a golden dragon,
Performing innumerable wonders of the dragon entirely at will.

When Master Hyanggok read it, he asked, "What would you do if a Garuda, which swallows dragons, suddenly appeared before you?"

Master Jinje answered, "Being cowered and disconcerted, I would withdraw three steps."

To this, Master Hyanggok was overjoyed saying, "That is Correct!"

Master Jinje shattered all of the *gongans* with ease, except for one about "Sun-faced Buddha and Moon-faced Buddha."

Master Jinje struggled with this *gongan* for about five years, and finally shattered it, after which he composed an enlightenment verse:

> With one strike of this Seon staff, the peak of Mt. Biro collapses,
> One thunderous roar crushes ten million Dharma teachings.
> In this small thatched hut, I lie down stretching my legs.
> A cool breeze over the ocean remains fresh for ten thousand years.

At the end of the 1967 three-month summer retreat, when he was 33 years old, Master Hyanggok and Master Jinje engaged in Dharma duel between.

Master Hyanggok ascended the Dharma seat and sat in silence for a while, at which point Master Jinje went forward and said,

"I don't want to ask about what all the Buddhas and the Patriarchs knew. However, I humbly ask you to speak a word of profound truth that all the Buddhas and the Patriarchs did not know."

"Nine times nine equals eighty-one," Master Hyanggok replied.

"That is a truth the Buddhas and Patriarchs already knew," Master Jinje said.

Master Hyanggok then said. "Six times six equals thirty-six,"

Without a word, Master Jinje bowed and withdrew. Without a word, Master Hyanggok descended from the Dharma seat and returned to his room.

The next day, Master Jinje visited Seon Master Hyanggok and asked again, "I'm not going to ask about the Buddha eye and the wisdom eye. However, what is the eye of this patched-robe monk?"

"The role of bhikkhunis (female monks) is supposed to be performed by women," Master Hyanggok said.

"Today I saw you in person for the first time," said Master Jinje.

"Where did you see me?" Master Hyanggok asked.

Master Jinje said, "Kwan (關)!"

Saying, "That's right, that's right!" Master Hyanggok then entrusted Master Jinje with the Dharma of the Linji lineage, gave him the new Dharma name Jinje, and bestowed on him a Dharma Transmission Verse. Master Jinje then became the 79th Dharma descendant of the Buddha. It was 1967, the Year of the Sheep.

Entrustment to Jinje Beopwon

The great living truth of the Buddhas and Patriarchs,

Can be neither given nor taken.

Now, I entrust this Dharma of the living phrase to you,

Whether you furl or unfurl the exhibit of Truth or release it is entirely up to you.

Hyanggok
August 10, 2993 B.E.

한중일 국제 무차선대법회, 해운정사, 2002

South Korea-China-Japan Great Equality Aseembly of Ganwha seon held at Haeunjeong-sa Monastery

간화선 수행법
(看話禪 修行法)

"부모에게 나기 전에 어떤 것이 참나인가?"

아침저녁으로 좌복 위에 반가부좌를 하고 앉아서 허리를 곧게 하고 가슴을 편 다음 두 손은 모아서 단전에다 붙입니다. 눈은 2미터 아래에다 화두생각을 두고 응시하되, 혼침과 망상에 떨어지지 않도록 눈을 뜨고 의심에 몰두해야 합니다.

이렇게 앉아서 무르익어지고 나면 일상생활 속에 가나오나 앉으나 서나, 일을 하나 산책을 하나, 잠을 자나 깨어

좌선
Sitting Meditation

서나 간절히 화두의심에 몰두해야 합니다.

이렇게 하루에도 천 번 만 번 '부모에게 나기 전에 어떤 것이 참 나인가?' 하고 오매불망 의심을 쭉 밀고 또 밀고 또 밀 것 같으면 모든 산란심이 일어날 틈이 없게 됩니다. 비유하자면, 시골의 방아 찧는 기계는 시동이 안 걸리면 방아를 못 찧는데, 한 번 시동이 걸리면 종일 방아를 찧을 수가 있는 것과 마찬가지입니다.

화두를 하루에도 천 번 만 번 의심을 밀어주라고 하는 이유는, 그렇게 천 번 만 번 의심하여 단련되면 문득 참의심이 시동 걸리게 되어 화두의심 한 생각이 끊이지 않고 지속되는 과정이 오기 때문입니다. 마치 흐르는 시냇물과 같이 밤낮으로 한 생각이 흐르고 흐르게 되는데, 앉아 있어도 밤이 지나가는지 낮이 지나가는지 모르게 되고, 보고 듣는 모든 것을 다 잊어버리게 됩니다.

그렇게 화두일념에 푹 빠져서 시간이 흐르고 흐르다가 사물을 보는 찰나에, 소리를 듣는 찰나에 홀연히 화두가 박살나게 되는 것입니다. 그러면 자신의 본래 면목이 드러나고 자연히 밝은 지혜의 눈이 열리어 억만년이 다하도록 항상 밝아 있게 되므로, 만인에게 진리의 지도자, 하늘세계와 인간세계의 사표(師表)가 되어 자유자재하게 활개를 치게 되는 것입니다. 이렇게 한 걸음도 옮기지 않고 마음의 고향에 이르면 멋진 자유와 행복과 세계 평화를 영원토록 누리게 되는 것입니다.

The Way of Ganhwa Seon

"What is your true self before you are born of your parents?"

Ganhwa Seon can be practiced whether you are an ordained monk or not. It can even be practiced with no previous knowledge of Buddhism.

In order to practice Seon, sit comfortably on your cushion in the morning and evening. Straighten your back, expand your chest, and place both hands on your lap below your navel. Look toward the floor six feet in front of you and focus your single-minded concentration on the *hwadu*. Keep your eyes open so that you don't succumb to drowsiness or distracting thoughts.

When your sitting Seon practice matures after some time, you must be able to focus on questioning your *hwadu*, not forgetting it for even a single moment. This should occur whether you're coming or going, sitting or standing, working or sleeping.

In this way, if you keep pushing forward again and again, raising questions tens of thousands of times about the *hwadu*, there will be no opportunity for any distraction to arise. For example, if the motor at a local mill is not turned on, it can't grind grain, but once the motor starts running, it will grind grain all day long. In the same way, I tell you to keep pushing forward with questions tens of thousands of times because once you become trained in this kind of questioning, you will suddenly reach the point of true questioning. The questioning of your *hwadu* will not cease for even a moment, but will flow continuously. This single-minded questioning will keep flowing day and night like a river. When you are sitting in Seon meditation you will be unaware of day or night; you will forget everything you see and hear. In this way, you become completely absorbed in the single-minded questioning of your *hwadu*. As time passes, there will ultimately come an instant when, upon seeing an object or hearing a sound, your *hwadu* will unexpectedly shatter.

At that point, your true self will be revealed and the eye of wisdom will open naturally and remain forever brilliant. You will then guide all people to the truth. As a great teacher in both the realms of heaven and humanity, you will be completely free and unhindered. In this way, when you reach the mind's home without having taken a single step, you will enjoy glorious freedom and happiness.